The Ultimate Guide to
ASSISTIVE TECHNOLOGY
IN SPECIAL EDUCATION

Resources for Education, Intervention, and Rehabilitation

D1122646

The Ultimate Guide to
ASSISTIVE TECHNOLOGY
IN SPECIAL EDUCATION

Resources for Education, Intervention, and Rehabilitation

JOAN L. GREEN

PRUFROCK PRESS INC.
WACO, TEXAS

Library of Congress Cataloging-in-Publication Data

Green, Joan L., 1963-
 The ultimate guide to assistive technology in special education : resources for education, intervention, and rehabilitation / Joan L. Green.
   p. cm.
 Includes bibliographical references.
 ISBN 978-1-59363-719-4 (pbk.)
 1. Communication devices for people with disabilities. 2. Assistive computer technology. 3. Self-help devices for people with disabilities. 4. Special education. I. Title.

 HV1568.4.G74 2011
 371.9'04334--dc22

                    2011002130

Edited by Lacy Compton

Production Design by Raquel Trevino

ISBN-13: 978-1-59363-719-4

Prufrock Press Inc.
P.O. Box 8813
Waco, TX 76714-8813
Phone: (800) 998-2208
Fax: (800) 240-0333
http://www.prufrock.com

TABLE OF CONTENTS

ACKNOWLEDGMENTS

I am grateful to:

- my husband, Mark Green, for his continuous love and support during this project;
- my children, Hallie, Ilana, Elise, and Aaron, for helping me explore some of the technologies that teenagers and students use daily and for all of their enthusiasm;
- my parents, Allan and Leah Lipman, and my brother, Bob Lipman, for always believing in me and offering creative suggestions;
- the many clients and families I have had the pleasure of working with who have put their faith in me to help them; and
- Rich Weinfeld, a special needs advocate and colleague, who suggested to me and Prufrock Press that we collaborate to write this book.

A NOTE TO THE READER

I wrote this book for you—parents, teachers, therapists, and individuals with communication, cognitive, literacy, and learning challenges. I hope that you find it helpful. I have done my best to include as many assistive technology resources as possible, but I know that as soon as I finish my final edits, this book will already not include all that could be helpful for you. Every effort has been made to make this guide as complete and accurate as possible. Websites are provided for the reader to refer to for up-to-date information.

Please use the resources in this guide as a starting point from which to learn more. I write a free online newsletter that I send to subscribers a couple of times a month. In it I highlight new products or technology ideas that you may find helpful. I also periodically offer webinars and seminars. If you'd like to receive the newsletter, please subscribe at either http://www.innovativespeech.com or http://www.ittsguides.com or e-mail me at Joan@innovativespeech.com, and I will add you to the list. I also post quite a bit of this new information on my Facebook page: Innovative Technology Treatment Solutions. It would be great if you could join that page.

As you read this book, please keep in mind that the information provided is not to be viewed as professional consultation or services. This guide was designed to provide information about helpful assistive technology tools that may potentially help individuals who have communication, cognitive, literacy, and learning challenges. It is not the purpose of this guide to provide training for professionals or prescribe evaluation or treatment protocols for clients. Anyone who decides to integrate technology into education and rehabilitation must expect to invest time and effort into exploring and trying the resources to learn which are best. Professional guidance is suggested.

CHAPTER 1
THE POWER OF TECHNOLOGY

CUTTING-EDGE TECHNOLOGY OFFERS NEW HOPE

As the affordability and availability of fantastic new multimedia tools that promote independence and personal, academic, and vocational success increase, so does the potential for greater success for people who have communication and cognitive challenges. Education and rehabilitation professionals, as well as families, need to develop new models of intervention and learn to adapt these cutting-edge technologies to empower individuals with literacy, learning, and communication differences. Unfortunately, many of the people who could benefit the most from these recent advances remain in paper-based worlds—receiving services that do not take advantage of effective new technology tools. People with disabilities are often never exposed to the many products that can help them succeed in life. As our society becomes increasingly dependent on technologies for communication and information access, people with disabilities are experiencing an ever-increasing digital divide. Everyone deserves to be exposed to affordable, easy-to-use resources with which they can accomplish everyday tasks more easily and effectively. The world of technology has become much more affordable—many state-of-the-art resources are now readily available and, when used properly, can have a huge positive impact on the lives of individuals with autism, learning differences, aphasia, cognitive deficits, and developmental as well as degenerative disabilities.

ASSISTIVE TECHNOLOGY

Assistive technology devices, also referred to as adaptive technology, according to the United States Assistive Technology Act of 1998 (see http://www.govtrack.us/congress/bill.xpd?bill=h108-4278), refer to any "item, piece of equipment, or product system, whether acquired commercially, modified, or customized, that is used to increase, maintain, or improve functional capabilities of individuals with disabilities" (Sec. 3.5). Assistive technologies can remove barriers to independence and success especially when used in the individual's natural setting such as his home, school, or workplace. These tools can reduce the burden of difficult skills and enhance independence during daily life at school, work, home, and in the community.

HELPFUL TECHNOLOGIES ARE ALL AROUND US

The worlds of assistive technology, educational technology, and mainstream technology are merging. This change is happening so fast that it is difficult to stay on top of the many new ways technology can be used to help people of all ages who have subtle or debilitating challenges. This guide will introduce you to an exciting world of assistive technology—one that includes many products and approaches that you may not know exist as well as many you may be very familiar with, but have not thought to use to help improve speaking, reading, writing, listening, thinking, memory, or learning skills.

TAKING THE FIRST STEP

Whether you are a parent of a child with communication, learning, or attention challenges, or a professional or caregiver of an adult who has had a stroke or head injury or suffers from a degenerative neurological disease, the keys to success in using this guide are the same:
- ✓ Start gradually.
- ✓ Focus on the sections within chapters that will meet your immediate needs first.
- ✓ Start to network with others in similar situations by joining online support and discussion groups.
- ✓ Explore the websites of products that seem most interesting to make sure that you learn about the most recent specifications, features, and price of the products.

✓ Take advantage of free trials before purchasing items and search online for reviews.

✓ Try out the many free resources described that may help.

✓ Be creative and try new things. There is no one correct way to proceed.

SEEK PROFESSIONAL GUIDANCE

This book does not replace the need for skilled professional intervention. Although assistive technologies are helpful in the education and therapy process, they do not replace specialized help from trained educators and therapists. Users of the technology need to remain focused on their goals and work to achieve the desired outcomes. Once a good match with the user and product is made, the selected resource should be configured or used in the best way to maximize progress toward goals. Some activities may be enjoyable, but aren't effective toward learning new skills. People learn in different ways and are helped by different strategies and types of assistance. Communication and cognitive professionals such as speech-language pathologists are trained to help people with communication and cognitive deficits, and computers are only a tool to further that help. One product can be used in many ways. Figuring out the most effective way to use the technology is critical for success.

TAKE ADVANTAGE OF
PRODUCT SUPPORT

Once you select software, adaptive hardware, or websites that will be potentially helpful for you in your setting, spend some time exploring the websites that are given for the products discussed. Many businesses offer free demo CDs, a trial period for online subscriptions, or online tutorials. If you go to a search engine such as Bing or Google and type in the name of the product and the word "reviews," you can often see what others have said about the product. Other helpful features offered by some companies are the ability to join an electronic mailing list, participate in chat sessions, receive free e-newsletters, or access a bulletin board that will connect you to other users of the product.

CHAPTER 2

THE BENEFITS OF ASSISTIVE TECHNOLOGY

WE NEED TO EMBRACE THE USE OF ASSISTIVE TECHNOLOGY TO HELP THOSE IN NEED

Technology has slowly crept into our lives. Assistive technology (AT) has become an integral part of this evolution and is gaining increased acceptance in the delivery of services in school and rehabilitation centers. Some professionals have welcomed this development of new resources to help others with open arms; some have avoided, resisted, or ignored these helpful tools; and others are unaware that new and exciting treatment opportunities exist.

Schools, healthcare systems, and vocational settings are struggling to balance the delivery of quality services with increasing costs. With the use of the assistive technologies highlighted in this guide, we become empowered to revolutionize the ability to contain costs and effectively help people of all ages with a wide range of communication, learning, and cognitive challenges. The key is to make a good match between the individual and the technology being used.

As technology continues to become more powerful, less expensive, and more portable, it becomes increasingly helpful in improving speech, language, new learning, reasoning, and memory. By creating opportunities as well as removing performance barriers, technology can help us explore new frontiers.

COMPUTERS ARE EVERYWHERE!

The use of computers in education and therapy first appeared in the late 1970s with the advent of microcomputers. Word processors gradually replaced typewriters. In the 1980s, computer use in education and therapy progressed to the use of drill-and-practice exercises with instant feedback to facilitate the learning process. The 1990s ushered in easier access to the Internet and more sophisticated software programs with voice output, the ability to customize options in programs for users, and more interesting and interactive software. Treatment started to incorporate the use of e-mail and websites for reading practice, research, and promotion of self-advocacy. Technology has continued to become more sophisticated and affordable. More and more people have high-speed Internet access and computers at home. Many students also have cell phones with texting and Internet access, iPods, iPads, and social networking accounts and are extremely computer savvy.

We are now in the midst of another technology transformation and need to change our mindset. The world of Web 2.0 has been around for a while with its emphasis on information sharing and collaboration. Some say Web 3.0 is just about here—with browsers that act like personal assistants. There is a growing emphasis on using products that are helpful to everyone, not just those with disabilities. There is a push toward a universal design for learning (UDL), created by the Center for Applied Special Technology (CAST; http://www.cast.org). UDL provides a "blueprint for creating flexible goals, methods, materials, and assessments that accommodate learner differences" (Kurzweil Education Systems, n.d., p. 1). In the world of assistive technology, there is also now more of an emphasis on helping instructors and employers learn to modify instruction and the workplace to find alternative ways to help students and employees demonstrate what they know.

DISABILITIES HINDER AN INDIVIDUAL'S ABILITY TO BENEFIT FROM MAINSTREAM COMPUTER USE

Communication and cognitive deficits create obstacles to computer use. As technology becomes even more important to mainstream society, people who do not have ready access to a computer or the Internet will be at an increasing disadvantage until the Internet and devices become more accessible to users with disabilities.

It may be difficult for individuals with communication and cognitive challenges to:

- ✓ provide computer input with movement of a mouse or typing on the keyboard,
- ✓ read and interpret information on the screen,
- ✓ sequence and analyze procedures needed to use software applications,
- ✓ use e-mail to obtain information and interact socially, and/or
- ✓ search online for information.

ASSISTIVE TECHNOLOGY OFFERS MANY BENEFITS

Appropriately selected assistive technologies can:

- ✓ save time;
- ✓ motivate;
- ✓ make tasks easier and often more fun;
- ✓ have real-life value;
- ✓ support unique learning styles, abilities, and backgrounds;
- ✓ provide feature flexibility and customizability at a level previously impossible;
- ✓ facilitate positive outcomes by carefully controlling tasks;
- ✓ give independent, nonjudgmental, immediate feedback;
- ✓ promote effective independent practice;
- ✓ streamline data and information collection;
- ✓ provide opportunities to objectively document change over time;
- ✓ increase opportunities for socialization and reduce isolation;
- ✓ provide more effective studying and learning strategies; and
- ✓ empower users to collaborate online.

MANY DIFFERENT TYPES OF PEOPLE CAN BENEFIT FROM ASSISTIVE TECHNOLOGY

Many new, powerful devices, software programs, and applications have been developed to help people confronted with a wide variety of challenges. People who are appropriate candidates for learning support from computers may have experienced or still have the following:

- ✓ a developmental delay or disorder;
- ✓ attention issues;

✓ autism;

✓ a learning disability;

✓ social, emotional, and behavioral challenges;

✓ developmental apraxia of speech;

✓ cognitive impairment;

✓ poor performance in school;

✓ work-related challenges;

✓ unintelligible speech (dysarthria);

✓ dysfluent speech (stuttering);

✓ difficulty learning English as a second language;

✓ a voice disorder;

✓ hearing impairment;

✓ low vision;

✓ a brain injury such as a stroke, a closed-head injury, a tumor, or an aneurysm;

✓ a progressive degenerative disease such as Parkinson's disease, amyotrophic lateral sclerosis (ALS), or multiple sclerosis (MS); or

✓ cognitive decline.

FAMILY ADVOCACY PUSHES PROFESSIONALS TO LEARN ABOUT AVAILABLE RESOURCES

Often the family members of people with disabilities take the initiative to learn more about educational methods and treatment options. They expect teachers and therapists to use state-of-the-art tools and methods. These family members confront the devastating impact every day that the disability imposes on many aspects of daily living and are very motivated to seek alternative solutions to maximize progress and quality of life.

This guide streamlines the learning process and makes it less daunting for professionals to offer assistive technology as a tool in their sessions. Educators and clinicians who understand what these new tools can do in solution-focused therapy to supplement other techniques can achieve excellent results. Incorporating affordable technology into rehabilitation and education is well worth the effort, time, motivation, and dedication it requires. This guide highlights software, hardware, and other resources that are versatile and therapeutically and educationally beneficial.

Technology Advances Continue

The items mentioned in this guide are not an exhaustive list of instructional tools and strategies, but rather a representative sampling of products available on the market and some suggestions about how to use them. The information presented is current at the time this book was written. However, it is inevitable that more products will become available and items described will change. New and improved features of software and apps are made available on a daily basis. Use the information included in this book as a guide for learning more and to perhaps point you in a direction to pave the way for you to take the initiative to learn how assistive technology can help you in your situation.

Software Can Quickly Provide Compensatory Strategies to Greatly Improve a Variety of Abilities

Some of the compensatory strategies software can provide include:

✓ Text readers can provide instant support for individuals who have good auditory comprehension skills, but poor reading comprehension or visual perceptual deficits. The computer will read aloud and perhaps highlight or enlarge the text that is selected on the screen. Readers may then be able to enjoy an online newspaper, better understand a school assignment, read an e-mail from a friend, or scan a letter into a computer and have it read aloud.

✓ Voice-recognition software can help those who have difficulty writing. It enables individuals with relatively clear speech and intact cognition to talk and have the computer or a device such as the iPad or a BlackBerry phone type what they say.

✓ Graphic organizers can help people who have difficulty thinking of words and organizing written narrative by providing a means for them to brainstorm and represent their thoughts with images and visual support. There is software that can be installed on a computer or users can work online in the "cloud."

✓ Word prediction technology and online dictionaries are helpful for people who have difficulty thinking of words. Several products offer semantic linking so that a person who can't think of a word can type in a related word and gradually click on items to help find what he was trying to type or say.

✓ Digital calendars and organizers can help people who have problems keeping track of daily activities and have poor time management skills. These programs can be on a computer, online, or on a handheld device.

✓ A digital pen can record audio as a person writes in order to assist with recall of a lecture for a student who has trouble taking notes in class or to provide talking flashcards.

✓ Communication software can empower people who can't speak by allowing them to select pictures or words and have the device speak for them. Most of these products can be customized to meet the needs of the user and many offer a dynamic display so that people can zero in on what they are trying to communicate with a couple of clicks.

CHAPTER 3

COMPUTERS, SOFTWARE, APPS, AND ACCESS

HELPFUL PRODUCTS ARE BECOMING LESS EXPENSIVE

Computers can provide a new world of independence for people with physical, communication, or cognitive disabilities. Designing environments, products, and information to be easily used by the greatest number of people, with or without disabilities, has become much more prevalent in the development of technological products. This translates into mainstream technology that is more accessible and serves the different needs and personal preferences of many users, including people with communication and cognitive deficits. Many hardware options and mainstream products can now be modified to provide functional and more affordable alternatives for users with disabilities. Products created for mainstream society may be the perfect assistive technology device for a person who is unable to write or speak. There is a new push toward making devices more user-friendly, which translates into more affordable products due to the larger consumer market.

COMPUTER ACCESS

One of the first steps when using computers is to determine which method of computer access is the most appropriate. For individuals with physical and cognitive limitations, it may be important to try a variety of monitors, keyboards, direct selection devices, and even varied cursors that can be found in the accessibility options of operating systems. When an individual has multiple physical issues and may benefit from help with positioning, adapted switches, or another complex access issue, a multidisciplinary assistive technology team is ideal to establish the best method of computer access. A comprehensive evaluation should be performed in the setting where the person will most likely use the resources and with input from the members of an educational, rehabilitation, or vocational team. Once the individual has the appropriate setup, a strategy can be developed for the use of technology to improve and compensate for communication, cognitive, literacy, and community-based challenges.

GUIDANCE FOR COMPUTER ACCESS AND ASSISTIVE TECHNOLOGIES

Several products and a number of extremely helpful online articles and protocols are available to assist with determining the most appropriate way for an individual to access technology.

The SETT Framework: Critical Areas to Consider When Making Informed Assistive Technology Decisions
by Joy Zabala
http://www.fctd.info/webboard/displayResources.php?id=472
- The SETT Framework focuses on the student, the environment, the tasks, and the tools. It was produced to assist teams through a variety of activities needed to help students select, acquire, and use assistive technology devices and software.
- More information on the uses of SETT can be found at http://atto.buffalo.edu/registered/ATBasics/Foundation/Assessment/sett.php.
- Windows and Mac
- Free

The Wisconsin Assistive Technology Initiative (WATI)
http://www.wati.org/?pageLoad=content/supports/free/index.php
- This program was designed to increase the capacity of school districts to provide assistive technology services by making training and technical assistance available to teachers, therapists, administrators, and parents throughout Wisconsin as they implement the assistive technology requirements of IDEA.

- This initiative provides manuals, assessment forms, self-assessment tools, children's stories, and examples of many successful applications.
- Many helpful free resources are available on its website in English and Spanish.
- Windows and Mac
- Free

Compass
by Koester Performance Research
http://www.kpronline.com
- Compass software measures the user's skills during computer interactions.
- It is designed to help clinical and educational professionals perform computer access evaluations with their clients and students.
- Skills assessed include keyboard and mouse use, navigation through menus, and switch use.
- Windows
- $179.00 ·

SWITCH SOFTWARE

Some individuals with significant motor impairments need to obtain access to the computer with the use of switches and scanning. There are a broad range of switches available, from very inexpensive devices to one that is quite sophisticated. Matching the right switch to the abilities of the individual is incredibly important and professional help should be used.

Options exist for users who use a single switch to operate computer software. A single switch can interface with a computer to act as any single key or mouse function. People can also use multiple switches, giving access to more computer controls. Switch-friendly software programs offer special onscreen layouts with several choices. Users then use the switch to select desired choices when a highlighted box moves over items on the screen one after the other, until the student presses the switch to make a selection. This process is referred to as switch scanning.

The process of scanning involves many skills such as controlling the switch, paying attention to the pictures or sounds on the monitor, and watching what happens after the selection is made. Mounting of the switch, body positioning, and switch selection and setup all have to be considered.

When an individual is only able to access software via a single switch, software selection is more limited. Many of the products described in this guide are accessible for people who need to use a switch. More detailed guidance on the use of technology and potential software for these users can be found at the following websites:

✓ **Switch In Time**: http://www.switchintime.com—This website has quite a few free programs for both Windows and Macintosh platforms.

✓ **Judy Lynn Software**: http://www.judylynn.com—Judy Lynn produces a variety of switch software and very helpful guidance for people with special needs.

✓ **Don Johnston**: http://www.donjohnston.com—This site offers a variety of software available for purchase.

✓ **HelpKidzLearn**: http://www.helpkidzlearn.com—This is a collection of free software for young children and those with learning difficulties to play online.

✓ **Hiyah.net**: http://www.hiyah.net—This free software has a full variety of switch activities for learners with multiple or significant special needs.

✓ **Northern Grid**: http://www.northerngrid.org—SENSwitcher is a suite of free programs designed to help teach early skills to people with profound and multiple learning difficulties, those who need to develop skills with assistive input devices, and very young children new to computers.

✓ **RJ Cooper & Associates**: http://www.rjcooper.com—This company has developed a number of switches for computers as well as the iPad.

✓ **Shiny Learning**: http://www.shinylearning.co.uk—Products here can be accessed using a variety of input devices such as switches or the keyboard as well as the mouse.

COMPUTER OPERATING SYSTEMS AND SPECIFICATIONS

As time passes, computers improve, helpful features become more mainstream, and costs decrease. Most desktop and laptop computers purchased within the past 5 years should be sufficient for therapy use if there is enough free space on the hard drive. Even the least expensive new computers are typically more than adequate and may actually be better than top of the line products available just a year or two ago. However, new complex software products with voice recognition or extensive graphics do sometimes require significant amounts of memory and often function better with higher speed computers. Specific computer requirements for particular software products are listed on their websites.

There are now also new technologies on the market that can be helpful for people with communication and cognitive challenges, but have a different set of features. Netbooks, tablets, iPads, and smartphones are commonplace. Hybrids of these products are also becoming prevalent. It is important to understand their advantages and disadvantages when deciding what to use.

It can be helpful to consult with computer-savvy friends and colleagues when moving forward with technology purchases. Also, be sure to take a look at the many online resources when deciding how to move forward. There are many blogs, podcasts, e-newsletters, and other helpful tools to learn more about assistive technology. Many are listed throughout this guide or can be found through an online search. It's important to connect with others in similar situations for guidance and to be able to try products before investing a significant amount of money in them. Magazine reviews, such as those in *PC Magazine* (http://www.pcmag.com) and *Consumer Reports* (http://www.consumerreports.com), are often also insightful for learning about mainstream technologies.

COMPUTER OPERATING PLATFORMS

An operating system is the software on a device that manages the programs and determines what can be done by the user. It is very important to know what assistive technology you will want to use when deciding which device to purchase to make sure that they are compatible.

- ✓ **PCs (Personal Computers)**: When people use the term PC they are typically referring to a Windows-based computer. Its operating system for desktop and notebook computers has changed over the years—Windows XP, Vista, and now Windows 7.
- ✓ **Open Source**: There are also open source computer platforms that can be used on PCs such as Linux. These platforms are available for anyone to use, modify, and redistribute freely. The Linux operating system is beginning to catch on, but is beyond the scope of this guide.
- ✓ **Mac OS**: Apple computers are once again becoming increasingly popular due to their ease of use and innovations. The current operating system is now Snow Leopard for laptop and desktop computers.
- ✓ **Tablet PCs**: These use a number of different platforms, including Windows 7.

✓ **iPad**: This tablet Mac computer uses a modified version of the iPhone operating system, which is derived from the Mac operating system.

✓ **Smartphones**: These phones (cell phones with more advanced computing ability and connectivity) use entirely different operating systems from tablets, notebooks, and desktops. The iPhone, Android phone, Palm phones, and BlackBerry devices all have their own operating systems.

More and more products are becoming hybrid or web/cloud based and are therefore usable by more devices with a broader range of operating systems.

With all of these systems, users can adjust screen colors, contrast, resolution, text and icon size, visual sound alerts, cursor size, and cursor speed. Operating systems also generally include an onscreen keyboard, screen readers, text-to-speech capability, and magnifier programs. Instructions are most often located within the operating system's help menu. Website information is listed in this guide as products are reviewed. The sites specify the platforms their products are compatible with and the software and hardware requirements.

APPLE COMPUTERS/DEVICES

Apple includes assistive technology in its products as standard features. Apple computers offer built-in accessibility features such as a screen reader, magnification, and captioning of downloadable digital movies. Apple refers to these features collectively as Universal Access. More information can be found at http:/www.apple.com/accessibility.

PERSONAL COMPUTERS/MICROSOFT

Windows 7 is the current platform, but these seem to change every few years and many individuals are still using XP and Vista. Details and tutorials about its accessibility options can be found at the following website: http://www.microsoft.com/enable. All of the platforms offer built-in accessibility settings and programs that make it easier for computer users to see, hear, and use their computers.

In the Ease of Access Center, there is quick access for setting up the accessibility settings and programs included in Windows. You'll also find a link to a questionnaire that Windows can use to help suggest settings that you might find useful. Open the Ease of Access Center by clicking the Start button, clicking Control Panel, clicking Ease of Access, and then clicking Ease of Access Center.

Computer Format—Desktops, Notebooks, Tablets, Handhelds, and Portable Word Processors

Technology is available in a wide variety of formats, including desktops, laptops, netbooks, tablets, and handhelds and hybrids. Each type of computer has pros and cons. Most are now available with integrated touch screens, wireless Internet access (wifi), Bluetooth, and the capacity to accommodate adapted keyboards and other alternate input devices.

During the selection process, it is necessary to consider:
- ✓ the degree of mobility needed,
- ✓ compatibility with other computers the user may be using,
- ✓ the cost,
- ✓ the need for online access, and
- ✓ most importantly, the needs of the user and the tasks that will be required.

DESKTOPS

Desktop computers are the most versatile, offer the largest monitor and keyboard, can accommodate a wide range of assistive technologies, and often provide the greatest value for equivalent specifications. Desktops are typically used when there is one designated computer location, and when the user wants to use a computer for more than simple word processing and Internet use. They are typically more difficult to transport. Newer upscale versions offer integrated touchscreens and the central processing unit integrated into the monitor, which is more convenient for changing locations.

NOTEBOOKS/LAPTOPS

Notebook computers now have all of the functionality of desktop computers. The price gap has narrowed with equivalent desktop computers. Compared to a desktop alternative, they are easier to transport and store, but the monitor and integrated keyboards are typically smaller.
- ✓ When compared to tablets and handheld devices, their weight prevents them from being easily transported. They have longer initial startup times and often have shorter battery lives. The keyboards are smaller than those of desktops, which may make them difficult to use for people who have visual or manual dexterity issues.

✓ Accommodations can make notebook computers easier to use. Regular keyboards can be attached, alternate mice and trackballs can be used, and talking software can read aloud text shown on the monitor.

✓ An advantage of this type of computer over a desktop computer in education and rehabilitation is that it can be used during treatment sessions and then brought home for practice.

TABLET COMPUTERS

Tablet computers look like the screen of a laptop. They may run a different operating system than desktops or laptops.

✓ Instead of a conventional keyboard, tablets often have a touch-screen that is activated with a finger or special pen/stylus as well as an onscreen keyboard to navigate and add data directly onto the screen.

✓ It can be docked to a station in order to use a keyboard, CD/DVD drive, or other peripherals if desired.

✓ Tablet computers are easily transported compared to notebook computers, but are typically heavier than netbooks and handhelds.

✓ The iPad (http://www.apple.com) is a very popular tablet computer and quite a few clones have become available.

NETBOOKS

Netbooks emerged in 2007 as small, lightweight, and inexpensive laptop computers primarily to be used for general computing and accessing the Internet and using web-based applications. They were initially much smaller than laptops, did not have DVD drives, and had quite a bit less memory and speed. They typically had a hard time running the newest operating systems because they didn't have enough power. Over the past few years, the specifications of netbooks have merged with those of cheaper laptops. There are now "super compact netbook computers" that offer users most features of a larger computer, but are easier to type on than using a handheld/smartphone.

IPODS, CELL PHONES, AND POCKET PCS

BlackBerry phones, iPhones, Android phones, and Pocket PCs have become widely used for business, personal use, education, and rehabilitation. There are many products coming on the market that fall in this category and offer many benefits such as the following:

✓ They can be used to help with organization, data entry, task management, and augmentative communication.

✓ Due to their small size, they are great if used as a communication device or as a help with memory.
✓ Many accessories and applications (apps) are becoming increasingly available and are useful when users have intact vision and fine motor control. Accessories and special features such as portable full-size keyboards and text readers are available to make them easier to use.

There are accessibility features on the 16 and 32 GB model iPod touches only and on the third generation iPod touch, iPhone 3GS, iPhone4, and iPads. These features include voice over, voice control, high-contrast mode, mono audio, and up to five times zoom. For more information, go to http://www.apple.com/accessibility and click on the specific tool on which you would like information for the accessibility features.

Some advantages of these handheld devices include:
✓ Handhelds can be synced to a larger computer on which it is easier to enter data.
✓ Infrared beaming allows the transfer of data without cables or external services, and wireless Internet access is now available on most models.

Despite these benefits, small handheld devices are currently not appropriate for all users. There are several drawbacks:
✓ Good fine motor control and vision are needed.
✓ The devices can be easily misplaced.
✓ The small screen is difficult on the eyes when used for sustained viewing.

SELECTION DEVICES

There are a variety of peripheral devices that can be used to help people who have difficulty accessing the computer.

MOUSE

A standard mouse may be fine for most people with good hand control. However, many people with disabilities have impaired fine motor movements and find it difficult to see the movement of the cursor on the computer screen. Some people are unable to use their dominant hand due to weakness, paralysis, or coordination deficits. It takes practice to use a mouse with the nonpreferred hand. The use of a mouse may be confusing for people with significant cognitive deficits who may do better with a touch screen instead.

TRACKBALLS

Trackballs are often a good solution for individuals who have coordination difficulties with their hands because the cursor can be controlled with a finger. The device stays in one place as the user moves the ball. The BIGtrack is the largest trackball available. This large ball requires less fine motor control than a standard trackball and it is ruggedly built.

TOUCH SCREENS

Touch screens are becoming much more affordable and prevalent. They are activated by touching with a fingertip or stylus. This type of direct selection is often more effective and intuitive with younger children, older adults, or individuals with significant cognitive deficits. Touch screens can be attached to or integrated into the monitor itself. Various prices and types are available. Newer products such as the iPad and smartphones come with multitouch screens. There is an Apple app titled Splashtop that sells for $1.99 and offers remote access to desktop or laptop computers so that individuals can access their computer and its programs by touching the iPad screen.

SWITCHES

Technology is available to assist people with little or no use of their hands. People who have reliable movement of just about any part of their body can control the cursor on the screen. Reliable mouth movement or even eye gaze can control the computer. Special switches make use of at least one muscle over which the individual has voluntary control, such as the head, knee, or mouth. To make selections, users use switches activated by movement. People who have severe mobility impairments often can use scanning and Morse code for computer access. Vendors offering a wide variety of switches are http://www.enablemart.com and http://www.rehabmart.com. Switches for the iPad are available at http://www.rjcooper.com.

TACTILE SYSTEMS

Individuals who have very low vision/blindness may be able to benefit from tactile systems such as Braille for computer access. Two great resources to locate technology for the blind are http://www.nyise.org/vendors.htm and http://www.nfb.org.

KEYBOARDS

Keyguards and keyboard overlays are helpful accessories when needed. They can decrease the number of unwanted keystrokes due to someone with poor manual coordination hitting more than one key at a time, keep the mechanics of a keyboard safe from the effects of spills and drooling, and help those who struggle to identify the keys.

Expanded keyboards that have larger keys spaced farther apart can replace standard keyboards for people with limited fine motor control. Mini-keyboards provide access for those who have fine motor control, but lack the range of motion to use a standard keyboard. There are also keyboard trays with adjustable arms that can be purchased for individualized positioning of the client. Most operating systems include special features that can help with keyboard use. To access those features, study the accessibility options of your operating system.

SPEECH AND VOICE INPUT

Speech input provides another option for people with disabilities who have difficulty typing. Through voice-recognition technology, the user controls the computer or enters text by speaking into a microphone. Most systems need to be trained to recognize specific voices—although this is becoming a less cumbersome process as technologies improve. Some of these products are very difficult for clients to use who have communication and cognitive deficits. SpeakQ by Quillsoft (http://www.wordq.com) was produced to help people with disabilities benefit from voice-recognition technology. There are also inexpensive apps for the iPad such as Dragon Dictation, which is very easy to use for several sentences at a time.

ENVIRONMENTAL CONTROL

Voice input can also be used for environmental control with environmental control units (ECUs). Commands can be given for turning lights on and off, adjusting room temperatures, and operating appliances when coupled with an environmental control unit or program. For more information about this type of technology, check out http://www.abilityhub.com/speech/speech-ecu.htm and http://abilitynet.wetpaint.com/page/Environmental+Control.

HEADSETS AND MICROPHONES

Much of the software described in this guide is for recording and listening to speech. It is often a sound investment to purchase a good set of headphones with a built-in microphone for use with voice recording and voice-recognition software. External noise reduction features are helpful. If the user uses a hearing aid or is not comfortable with a headset, a desktop microphone can be purchased instead.

NETWORKS

The main benefit of a network is that it allows more than one computer to share resources such as Internet connections, storage space, printers, and applications.

✓ Remote access enables people to access a computer from different locations.

✓ Networks facilitate group collaboration, allowing the sharing of calendars, files, and even simultaneous sharing of applications.

✓ A downside to the use of networks is that they add a level of complexity and outside help may be needed to install, configure, and maintain them.

PROTECTION

Safeguards need to be in place to protect the computer and the personal information stored on it.

✓ Quality surge protectors are needed to avoid harm from thunderstorms and other electrical surges.

✓ Virus, spyware, and firewall protection keep the computer free of harmful external influences.

✓ Frequent software updates keep things running smoothly.

✓ Passwords should be used to prevent unauthorized access.

ADDITIONAL RESOURCES

There are many articles, blogs, YouTube videos, and websites that offer more information on the products mentioned above. Below are some resources to help you learn more about the selection and purchase of hardware and peripherals for assistive technology.

✓ **AbilityHub**: http://www.abilityhub.com

✓ **Apple Accessibility**: http://www.apple.com/accessibility

✓ **Assistivetech.net**: http://www.assistivetech.net

- ✓ **EnableMart**: http://www.enablemart.com
- ✓ **Mayer-Johnson**: http://www.mayer-johnson.com
- ✓ **Microsoft Accessibility**: http://www.microsoft.com/enable
- ✓ **Madentec**: http://www.madentec.com
- ✓ **Pass It On Center**: http://www.passitoncenter.org
- ✓ **Rehabtool.com**: http://www.rehabtool.com
- ✓ **Rigel Technology**: http://www.atechcenter.net
- ✓ **RJ Cooper & Associates**: http://www.rjcooper.com

CHAPTER 4

TECHNOLOGY TO IMPROVE VERBAL EXPRESSION

This chapter highlights assistive technologies that can be used to enhance verbal expression. A multimedia approach using sound, text, and pictures helps with verbal communication. Prior to the selection of products, it's essential to analyze the major obstacles of speaking and figure out what is needed to improve it. In addition to exploring the use of technology to assist with improved talking, it is also important to use conventional strategies for helping people who struggle to make themselves understood. Simple steps such as providing additional response time, loading the environment with resources with which to refer when communicating, and accepting shortened or alternative types of responses can help. People appreciate being given enough time to formulate and to speak their thoughts.

Verbal expression deficits can be the result of motor, structural, and pragmatic impairments from issues such as:

- ✓ developmental delay,
- ✓ language and learning disability,
- ✓ cleft palate,
- ✓ autism,
- ✓ foreign accent,
- ✓ learning English as a second language,
- ✓ hearing loss,
- ✓ voice disorder,
- ✓ head injury,
- ✓ aphasia,

✓ apraxia,

✓ dysarthria,

✓ dementia,

✓ progressive neurologic disease, or

✓ intubation.

Many specialized software programs, as well as mainstream products, can be used to help both children and adults with a wide variety of needs. A large number of resources are available to help improve articulation, word retrieval, sentence formulation, and dialogue. Some products are very structured, provide feedback, and are intuitive in terms of the increasing level of difficulty. There are also software programs designed to augment communication.

SOFTWARE PROGRAM CHARACTERISTICS FOR SPEECH GOALS

People who have dysarthria (slurred speech), a heavy foreign accent, verbal apraxia (speech-motor programming problems), developmental articulation errors, or impaired speech due to a hearing impairment can benefit from software products for improving speech patterns.

Features of these products may include:

✓ a focus on the production of particular sounds grouped by sound or in functional context in words, phrases, and sentences;

✓ a desciption of how to physically form sounds using text and diagrams;

✓ pictures and videos of up-close mouth movements;

✓ recordings of the sounds for users to listen to and repeat (may be helpful for people who can't perceive the accuracy of their response or a hindrance for people who find it distracting);

✓ the ability to convert the speech to text;

✓ feedback on the accuracy of the user's speech; and

✓ computer-based visual biofeedback in graphic representations for pitch, volume, intonation pattern, easy onset of phonation, and articulatory precision.

TEXT READERS AND TALKING WORD PROCESSORS

In addition to using software that features drill-and-practice techniques to improve speech sound production, the use of text readers and talking word processors (discussed later in this book) can be very helpful. Word and sentence lists can be written into documents that the computer reads aloud. Users can practice reading aloud and then listen to the computer for help as needed or to check their responses.

SOFTWARE PROGRAM CHARACTERISTICS FOR LANGUAGE GOALS

People who have aphasia, word-retrieval problems, delayed language, or who are learning English as a second language need to work on thinking of words as well as saying them. They also need to practice using words in phrases or sentences to convey meaning. Software products that are helpful for improving expressive language focus on tasks involving confrontation naming, repetition, sentence formulation, and dialogue. The stimuli are often arranged by topic or situation rather than sounds. Some use text only, some use pictures alone or pictures with text, and others have authoring capability, so that the user can use personalized information to practice.

Many moderately impaired people are able to communicate their basic needs and wants, repeat long sentences, and name basic pictures. These individuals may have difficulty communicating more complex desires, retrieving words, and formulating sentences or abstract thoughts. When working with people whose disabilities are more subtle, it is helpful to focus on challenging tasks such as:

- ✓ recalling less common words or those with a cognitive component such as opposites or analogies;
- ✓ formulating novel sentences to describe complex pictures, steps in a task, or solutions to problems; and
- ✓ engaging in dialogue for conversation-level practice.

ASSISTIVE STRATEGIES AND TECHNOLOGY FOR BASIC VERBAL EXPRESSIVE NEEDS

People who have had significant developmental delays, autism, or congenital problems; a severe stroke or head injury; vocal surgery; intubation; or who have limited English proficiency may have severe verbal expression problems. If a person is unable to convey basic thoughts and needs, an appropriate first goal is to find a way for him to express his basic needs and wants. It is necessary to analyze the following factors:

- ✓ the person's initiative in attempting to communicate;
- ✓ the frequency, range of intent, and effectiveness of messages being communicated nonverbally;
- ✓ the effect of cognitive, motor, and/or sensory impairments on the person's ability to learn and use nonverbal communication methods; and

✓ the resourcefulness of the communication partner to stimulate communication and understand what's expressed by the individual.

VOICE OUTPUT DEVICES

Voice output devices are also referred to in the literature as augmentive and alternative communication (AAC), augcom, and voice output communication aides (VOCA). Once an individual is able to indicate his basic needs with the help of his communication partner, the next step is to consider devices that may enable him to be more independent in his ability to select a picture or word on a communication board, in a book, or one said aloud by a device.

It is helpful to look at the person's ability to generate novel verbal utterances rather than just selecting one item with the use of either pictures or words. There are low-level papers and books that picture basic need items, while others offer more words, and are also more visually complex. Voice output devices may provide a single layer of items for direct selection, while others provide multiple layers through dynamic display. Picture communication dictionaries; apps on an iPad, iPod touch, or smartphone; several of the talking Franklin-brand products; calendars; talking photo albums; and address books on cell phones can also assist with communication.

People who have more of a motor-based speech problem or impaired communication due to muscular weakness generally respond favorably to the functional use of communication books and talking communication devices. Individuals who have severe language-based problems such as aphasia or severe cognitive deficits that interfere with talking, tend to not functionally respond as well to the use of communication devices. People with severe aphasia and learning issues have difficulty sequencing concepts to express their thoughts and needs. Often in such cases, it's the resourcefulness and ability of the communication partner to facilitate communication that determines the effectiveness of the assistive device or communication book.

Children who have not yet developed language may benefit from these items in the process of learning language. Extensive training for both adults and children is required.

CUSTOMIZATION

Technology must be individualized and used in ways to meet the needs of a person with communication challenges, but technology alone will not cure a long-term problem. These state-of-the-art devices and approaches should be used in conjunction with other effective methods of treatment and the input of a trained professional. Technology needs will continue to change as the needs of the individual changes.

COMPUTER SOFTWARE TO HELP
IMPROVE VERBAL EXPRESSION

Different software programs provide different ways of assisting with or compensating for verbal expression challenges. The websites for each described product are given to provide you with information that is more detailed regarding versions of the software, networking ability, preferred operating systems, and availability of online tutorials or demos. The prices written in this guide are generally for an individual home version of each item. These prices will undoubtedly change, but they are included to give a ballpark estimate. Most programs are suitable for both children and adults unless specifically indicated.

This listing is not all-inclusive, but it is a good place to start. Several programs are listed more than once. This was done to simplify the process when searching for software that uses a particular approach.

As you read this list, keep in mind the features that are most helpful to a particular person:

- ✓ **Close-up video of mouth movement**: This is often most helpful for people with verbal apraxia, which is a motor coordination problem.
- ✓ **Pictures, text, and sounds of common words**: When people are exposed to the multisensory stimulation of seeing pictures and words, reading text, and hearing words said aloud, new learning is enhanced.
- ✓ **Pictures and words shown in natural settings**: It is often helpful for people with language deficits to see pictures of items in context or grouped by category. In addition to using the following programs to create drill-and-practice opportunities for language activities, a creative therapist, parent, or teacher might be able to encourage the individual to use the programs listed in this chapter to facilitate communication.
- ✓ **Practice on specific speech sounds**: Users can listen to recordings of words and phrases as often as needed. Speech can be recorded and played back for comparison to the recorded computer voice. These programs are very helpful for people who have apraxia and dysarthria, as well as for people who are working on improving clarity and fluency of connected speech. Software to help with articulation of specific sounds can be divided into two distinct groups: Some programs are produced for people with special needs, while others are produced for foreign accent reduction.

> ▶ The software designed for special needs is typically very intuitive and uses large text and graphics. These programs are often easy for individuals to use for independent practice. There is generally helpful phone support as needed.
>
> ▶ Products designed for accent reduction are typically more visually challenging for people with visual-perceptual issues.

✓ **Authoring capability**: Programs that offer the ability to customize the stimuli items are helpful for learning to say personalized information and for creating practice materials that are relevant for each person.

✓ **Cognitive components**: People with subtle deficits are often quite capable of performing straightforward language tasks, such as repeating sentences and naming pictures; however, when reasoning and memory components are added to the task, performance deteriorates. Deficits are often exacerbated when people are asked to describe solutions to problems, complete analogy tasks, or summarize written material. As tasks become more abstract, the response becomes more difficult.

✓ **Text readers**: Text-reading software reads text aloud from the computer. The multisensory input can be very helpful when working to improve verbal expression. Word lists, phrases, and sentences can be read aloud.

✓ **Topic-based sentences, dialogue tasks, and programs encouraging verbal narrative**: Many individuals with verbal expression deficits need help establishing carryover with new articulatory patterns, fluent speech, word retrieval strategies, and the organization of content in connected discourse. A computer can be used as a context for this type of practice in many ways. The parents, teacher, therapist, or a computer buddy can provide communication models and work toward verbal communication goals while using engaging activities with the client on the computer.

✓ **Visual or graphic feedback of speech and voice production**: Some people are very motivated when they see something happen on the screen when they verbally produce something correctly.

✓ **Voice recognition**: Software with voice recognition will type what the user dictates. This in itself can be quite motivating for the production of accurate verbal production. There is also some software that "grades" whether or not speech is produced correctly rather than just recording it for playback.

Available products are listed in three categories:

1. software to load onto a computer or that plays from a CD/DVD,
2. online programs, and
3. apps that can be used on mobile devices.

SOFTWARE TO LOAD ONTO A COMPUTER OR THAT PLAYS FROM A CD/DVD

American Speechsounds
by Speechcom
http://www.speechcom.com

- This program is very helpful for improving articulation of specific speech sounds.
- It includes more than 8,000 words and expressions, as well as consonants and vowels, with video and audio.
- Recordings can be made, immediate feedback is provided, and performance scores are documented.
- Lessons offer practice with fluency, intonation, and distinguishing between correctly and incorrectly produced sounds and words.
- Video clips, diagrams, instructions, explanations of common problems, and spelling examples are presented for every sound.
- There are personal and professional versions available.
- Windows
- $74.95 for the personal version

Articulation I, II, and III
by Learning Fundamentals
http://www.learningfundamentals.com

- Stimuli are grouped by speech sound.
- Users can practice saying sounds, words, phrases, and sentences.
- Digitized speech presents stimuli in normal or exaggerated speech models.
- Onscreen recording and playback are provided for immediate feedback.
- Articulation I focuses on consonant phonemes, Articulation II works on consonant clusters, and Articulation III works with vowels plus /R/ and /r/ clusters.
- Windows and Mac
- $99.00 for each program

Clicker 5

by Crick Software

http://www.cricksoft.com

- This software contains a set of grids on the bottom half of the screen. Words, phrases, or pictures can be placed in the cells of the grid.
- The program includes thousands of pictures, and the grids are easy to produce.
- The lessons are either set up by the parent, clinician, or teacher or downloaded from http://www.learninggrids.com. The majority of the sets are designed for students from preschool onward. However, there is a category for adult learners that contains some sets that can be adapted and used by adults.
- Digital photos as well as video clips of items in a house or family members can be used.
- The user can right click on the pictures or words in the grid to have the computer say aloud what was recorded for that cell.
- When the cells in the grid with words or pictures are selected with a left mouse click, the contents of the cell are moved to a talking word processor on the top half of the screen.
- Several cells can be selected to form sentences. When final punctuation is used, the computer reads the sentence aloud.
- Windows and Mac
- $249.00

Dudsberry's Fishing Fun

by Janelle Publications

http://www.janellepublications.com

- Children are engaged in the adventures of a dog named Dudsberry who is asleep in his doghouse, then roused by a storm. His photo album is blown away and the activities help him rebuild his album.
- A fishing game is used to practice saying the phonemes: r, l, s, and r, l, and s blends.
- Speech skills can be practiced at the word, sentence, and spontaneous speech level.
- Windows and Mac
- $39.00

The Great Action Adventure

by Silver Lining Multimedia

http://www.silverliningmm.com

- Skills taught include receptive noun and verb matching, sign language, word matching, and verb tenses.

- This software is most appropriate for children.
- It includes full-motion video of verbs and sign language.
- The lessons are customizable with both play and learning areas. The parent or educator selects which words are taught, how they are presented, and how the student is reinforced and prompted.
- Windows and Mac
- $69.95

"It's a . . ." Bundle: Therapy for Expressive Naming Disorders
by Learning Fundamentals
http://www.locutour.com/products/product.php?id=7

- The first program has 100 pictures of food, 100 pictures of everyday objects, 100 mixed pictures, 120 pictures of animals in their habitats, and 25 pictures of Spanish foods.
- The program "And a One, Two, Three" focuses on syllable segmentation practice.
- There are a variety of cueing strategies to provide both visual confrontation and responsive naming tasks.
- Voice can be recorded.
- Windows and Mac
- $99.00

LanguageLinks: Syntax Assessment and Intervention
by Laureate Learning Systems
http://www.laureatefamily.com

- LanguageLinks takes users from the early two-word development stage through the mastery of a broad range of syntactic forms.
- Six levels train more than 75 essential grammatical forms in developmental order.
- The software begins with an assessment to determine where to start training. Then the program tracks detailed information about performance and automatically guides the user through the curriculum.
- Windows and Mac
- $97.50

Looking for Words
by Attainment Company
http://www.attainmentcompany.com

- This program presents three different settings to explore: the home, the town, and the school.

- The cursor turns into a magnifying glass in the explore mode. It is possible to enter different rooms in a house and go to different streets in a town. Once in a location, an item is selected and then highlighted. The text is printed in large letters while the item is named aloud.
- This software offers a task in which the user finds items on a list, which involves memory, sequencing, and reasoning. Verbal expression skills can be practiced during this task by having clients verbalize where they are going, why, and what they will do next to find items on the list.
- Windows and Mac
- $99.00

My House, My Town, and My School:
The Language Activities of Daily Living Series
by Laureate Learning Systems
http://www.laureatefamily.com

- These programs offer house, town, and school environments in which children and adults learn about objects and activities encountered in daily living routines.
- Each program includes six scenes to teach more than 100 common vocabulary items.
- There are four activities for each scene. The user can click on an object, and the computer says its name or function. There are also activities in which the program asks the user to find the location of a named or described object.
- Windows and Mac
- $97.50 per program for families

My School Day
by Silver Lining Multimedia
http://www.silverliningmm.com

- My School Day uses real-life video to take the child into a typical school day, including the classroom, cafeteria, and playground.
- It provides an opportunity for students to view appropriate interactions and social behaviors within the school environment.
- The user is asked to identify, produce, and explain several social situations in response to the video, which is embedded in interactive software.
- Progress can be charted.

- It's appropriate for children with the cognitive ages of 6–15 years old.
- Windows and Mac
- $89.99

Say-N-Play
by Advance Games
http://www.saynplay.com
- This program uses speech recognition to improve articulation.
- Children speak through a headset microphone to interact with the game.
- In a lesson mode, the user selects a sound to work on and decides which game he wants to play. The program automatically adjusts the level of difficulty based on performance—the quality of the sound utterance.
- While in free play mode, the target productions are selected by the computer.
- Words are presented both in written and picture format, which also helps to develop reading skills.
- Multiple levels are available and progress reports track success.
- Windows
- $129.00 for the home version with three player profiles

SentenceShaper 2
by Bungalow Software
http://www.bungalowsoftware.com
- Users record utterances and then arrange the recordings into phrases, sentences, and stories.
- In the pro and editing version, users can record descriptions of their photos in computer scrapbooks.
- There are more than 800 screens of therapy material that provide practice on different kinds of sentences of increasing complexity.
- No reading or typing is required to use the program.
- It can be used for speech practice or as a communication aid.
- Windows
- $399.50 for the home version; $649.50 for the Pro+editing version

Sights 'n Sounds 1
by Bungalow Software
http://www.bungalowsoftware.com
- This program has six lessons and more than 400 words.

- Sections include single-syllable words, short words organized by beginning sound, short words organized by ending sound, pictures and words for nouns, pictures and words for verbs, and words for abstract concepts.
- There is an authoring component to this program. This is a very helpful feature so that users can practice saying personal information such as the names of family and friends, important phrases, home phone numbers, and addresses.
- The program has an easy-to-use interface with little visual distraction.
- A Spanish version is available.
- Windows
- $159.50 for the individual deluxe user with editing
- Also available for $50.00 a month when used where Internet access is available. The software is loaded onto a computer but the subscription is verified online.

Sights 'n Sounds 2
by Bungalow Software
http://www.bungalowsoftware.com

- This program helps users speak phrases or sentences by prompting them with a picture, text, or model sentence.
- Users can add specialized conversational phrases, parts of speeches, or phrases for common activities.
- Windows
- $159.50 for the individual deluxe user with editing
- Also available for $50.00 a month when used where Internet access is available. The software is loaded onto a computer but the subscription is verified online.

Sound Beginnings—Making Sounds
by Tool Factory
http://www.turningpointtechnology.com

- Making Sounds is the third edition of this unique vocalization program, designed to encourage communication in young children and those with special education needs.
- Using a microphone, the user follows directions and controls the actions of characters on the screen.
- The teacher options include printable student records, configuration controls for speed and frequency, and the ability to import pictures and photos within the jigsaw activity.

- Voice-activated activities include counting, flying the bird, painting with noise, racing with sustained sounds and volume, and placing words.
- Windows and Mac
- $69.95

SpeechPacer
by Bungalow Software
http://www.bungalowsoftware.com
- The program teaches users to speed up or slow down speech to improve intelligibility.
- Reading material is shown on the screen, and a reading cursor highlights text for the user to read aloud.
- The rate of highlighting, the amount of text shown at once, and whether the cursor is advanced automatically or manually can be customized.
- $69.50 for the home version

Speech Sounds on Cue
by Bungalow Software
http://www.bungalowsoftware.com
- The user first selects the target sound for practice. The software then provides drill and practice on words beginning with that sound in a sentence completion task with text, sound, picture, and mouth movement.
- The program records and plays back the user's voice for comparison, and there is now an option to randomize the order of stimuli presentation.
- The up-close video of mouth movement is especially helpful for users with apraxia.
- This program was recently updated. The new version has a North American voice.
- Windows and Mac
- $149.50 for home use
- $50.00 as part of a monthly subscription.

Talk Now English (American)
by EuroTalk
http://www.eurotalk.com
- This product was actually designed to teach English as a second language.

- To work on verbal expression skills, the user first selects a category. Categories include basic phrases, colors, numbers, food, shopping, and time. Users can practice repeating and naming pictured items.
- There are hundreds of items to practice in a game format and several ways to work on saying the names of pictures. Users can name items and then click to hear the word and compare it to the correct production. There is also a game in which users name a set number of items in a row and then record their utterances.
- This software is available in 102 languages.
- Windows and Mac
- $34.99

TalkTime With Tucker
by Laureate Learning Systems
http://www.laureatefamily.com

- This voice-activated program is most appropriate for encouraging children with speech impairments to vocalize.
- When the child talks or makes sounds into the microphone, Tucker moves and talks. This program accepts a broad range of sounds and speech to make Tucker come alive. Almost any input is followed by an appropriate response.
- There are activities to teach cause and effect, turn-taking, animal sound imitation, increasing verbalization length, changing voice volume, and natural communication exchanges.
- Windows and Mac
- $62.50 for family edition

The Talking Series
by Laureate Learning Systems
http://www.laureatefamily.com

- There are three programs in this series—Talking Nouns I, Talking Nouns II, and Talking Verbs—with about 50 stimuli each.
- The teacher, therapist, or parent first selects the words to be provided and the nature of the task.
- With the "interactive communication" selection, the computer can either be set to say each word as it is selected or to speak only after a phrase or sentence has been completed. In both cases, the computer adds articles and verb inflections so that only grammatically correct phrases are heard.
- In the picture-matching task, a picture appears on the monitor and the user is asked to find its match.

- In the picture-identification task, the computer names a picture and the user finds it.
- Animation is provided on the Talking Verbs CD.
- Windows and Mac
- $75.00 for families for each program

Tell Me More
by Auralog
http://www.tellmemore.com

- The Virtual Conversation activity engages users in an interactive conversation environment featuring a variety of characters.
- This program is divided into six workshops, including grammar and vocabulary.
- It has an oral, dynamic mode with real-time performance analysis and a guided mode.
- Speech recognition technology evaluates pronunciation and detects and corrects errors and 3-D animations illustrate the movements of the lips and mouth.
- $229.00 for two levels

Tiger's Tale
by Laureate Learning Systems
http://www.laureatefamily.com

- This program is most appropriate for use with children. It stimulates language production by encouraging students to talk for a tiger who has lost his voice. Preschool and elementary students are motivated by recording their voices to create their own movies.
- During the tiger's search, animated characters appear and ask children questions to elicit their thoughts, suggestions, and opinions.
- These "home" movies, which can be saved for future viewing, are enjoyable to watch and can help measure progress over time.
- Windows and Mac
- $62.50 for family edition

WordQ+SpeakQ
by Quillsoft
http://www.st4learning.com

- The SpeakQ voice-recognition product is an add-on to WordQ software.
- It was developed for users with mild to moderate communication and cognitive deficits.

- This can be used at any time the user has the choice of typing with the keyboard, using word prediction software, or speaking straight into the text.
- Speech recognition and word prediction are integrated to enhance the effectiveness of each other.
- Windows and Mac
- $279.00

World Talk English (American)
by EuroTalk
http://www.eurotalk.com

- There are interactive games to improve fluency and comprehension with vocabulary relating to food, weather, and animals.
- Exercises enable users to work on writing words and sentences, dictation, following directions, formulating sentences, and using numbers.
- A "recording studio" can be used for practicing verbal expression, sentence construction, and word retrieval, and a simulated TV quiz targets comprehension skills.
- This software is available in many languages.
- Windows and Mac
- $39.99

ONLINE PROGRAMS

Online programs are available to either PC or Mac users unless otherwise indicated.

Alexicom Tech
by Alexicom Tech
http://www.alexicomtech.com

- Alexicom Tech is an AAC delivery system via the Internet. Users of this system can use a computer, cell phone, or other Internet-capable device.
- The parent or teacher accesses language templates, pictures, and icons via the Alexicom Tech site; creates pages; and downloads them to a computer or handheld device, which may then be used anywhere.

- Alexicom Tech is designed to be extremely user-friendly and has the ability to grow with the user as his or her needs change.
- $40.00 a month

Parrot Software
by Parrot Software
http://www.parrotsoftware.com

- Parrot Software offers approximately 70 programs designed to improve communication and cognition as part of an online subscription.
- There are a large number of programs from which to choose that are grouped into categories, and the website helps users select appropriate programs.
- A number of the programs use voice recognition—the user speaks and makes things happen based on the accuracy of the verbal production.
- A Spanish Internet subscription is available.
- Phone support is excellent.
- An online subscription for an indiviual is $24.95 a month. Programs can also be purchased separately on CDs.

**Pronunciation Power 1, Pronunciation Power 2,
and 8 in 1 English Dictionary**
by English Learning
http://www.englishlearning.com

- Stimuli are grouped by speech sounds.
- Both front and side views are shown for all of the 52 sounds at normal speed and in slow motion.
- Drill-and-practice exercises are given for more than 7,000 words at the word and sentence levels.
- After a sound is presented, it's followed by speech analysis activities, lessons, and four different kinds of exercises, sample words, comparative words, listening discrimination, and sentences.
- 8 in 1 English Dictionary offers translations in 12 languages and more than 2,000 pictures and graphics. Users can listen to and record more than 7,000 words, including plurals of nouns and conjugations of verbs. There are 10 different ways to search for words including by themes such as animals, colors, and clothing; by the location of the sound in a word; or by whether it is a verb or a noun.
- Windows
- $49.70 for 3-month online subscription

TapToTalk

by Assistyx LLC

http://www.taptotalk.com

- The TapToTalk web app works with netbooks, tablet PCs, touch-screens, or any Internet-connected computer.
- The TaptoTalk Designer includes more than 2,400 images to customize this augmentative communication system that can be delivered using apps on the Nintendo DS and Apple and Android devices.
- Words, phrases, and sentences will be spoken when the child taps on the picture.
- Voices can be recorded to be said when pictures are selected.
- Personalized albums of pictures can be used on one or more devices with the free apps.
- $99.95 a year

VizZle

by Monarch Teaching Technologies

http://www.monarchteachtech.com

- VizZle is web-based customizable software for AAC and visual learning.
- It was created to help children with autism, but it is helpful for a wide range of users.
- It has a searchable library of lessons that range from academics to personal hygiene, matching boards, game boards, interactive books, and a visual language lab that can be interactive and customizable.
- There are three core areas—creation of the communication boards, a teaching and filing system, and a library in which to share the material.
- Contact the company for a cost quote, which is a monthly based subscription. There is a special discount for parents.

APPS THAT CAN BE USED ON MOBILE DEVICES

Be sure to check the iTunes store so that your device is compatible with the particular app and to view the most recent features and pricing. Some apps only work with newer models. It is also very helpful to read users' reviews prior to purchase and to look at other apps people have purchased. Many apps that are relatively expensive have lite versions to try before purchasing the fully featured version. There are often instructional videos on the website of the company that produces the app to assist new users in learning about features and how to use the product. To purchase Apple apps, users need to download the iTunes software for free at http://www.iTunes.com and configure it to work with their device or purchase the app directly from the device.

Please keep in mind that many of the apps listed can be used in creative ways to maximize their effectiveness. Try not to look at the app as a static product and only use it in the way that it was developed to be used. For instance, merely looking at a flashcard will not be as effective at stimulating language as it would be if a parent, teacher, or therapist turns it into a more interactive experiential activity. An individual who needs help with social skills may benefit from using apps in a group situation to improve turn-taking or conversational skills.

ABA Flashcards

by Kindergarten.com

http://www.kindergarten.com

- Apple app
- Kindergarten.com created 24 sets of Applied Behavior Analysis (ABA) flashcards with colorful, concrete, high-quality photos of items, objects, people, actions, and concepts that are easy to understand. Each set is a different app.
- Some of the sets are grouped by topics like emotions, shapes, and actions and can be used to improve word recall and articulation.
- There are also apps that require problem-solving skills in which the user must choose among three or four choices. These apps can be used to generate sentences and conversation.
- Many of the apps are free and some cost $0.99

Articulate it!

by Smarty Ears

http://www.smartyearsapps.com

- Apple app
- The app includes all sounds in the English language and more than 1,000 pictures that can be grouped according to manner of articulation or phonological process.
- It provides detailed scoring records.
- Users can record their voices and compare speech sounds to the recording.

- The app allows parents or therapists to take notes during practice sessions.
- Multiple students can be tracked at once on different goals.
- $34.99

ArtikPix
by RinnApps
http://rinnapps.com/artikpix/Home.html

- Apple app
- ArtikPix includes 20 card decks that each include 40 cards for the following sounds: f, v, ch, sh, k, g, s, z, l, r, s-blends, l-blends, r-blends, p, b, m, n, t, d, and j.
- Each deck has three levels of matching activities to address articulation difficulties.
- Cards show pictures and text and can say each word aloud if configured to do so. If an arrow is selected, the words are used in a sentence.
- Users are prompted to practice and record their verbalizations.
- Individuals tap and flick cards to practice their sounds in fun activities.
- Data can be collected, saved, and shared to e-mail, clipboard, or the Google Spreadsheet application.
- Decks can be combined or configured in ways to facilitate progress.
- A free app is available with just the "th" deck.
- $29.99 for the complete program

AutoVerbal Talking Soundboard PRO
by No Tie, LLC
http://www.notiesoftware.com

- Apple app
- AutoVerbal allows kids with autism and people who are nonverbal to communicate using hundreds of picture buttons including buttons to speak many preprogrammed messages.
- There are a variety of topics presented in rows such as medical, food, and emotions. Users tap on the picture to have a word or phrase said aloud. The first row is for customizable utterances that the user can program in the custom mode found in the help menu.
- Premium voices can be used with the device when it is online but responses are slower. Otherwise, a fairly robotic-sounding voice is used.
- Type text and it will be spoken aloud.

- Users can hold the device sideways to see a log of recent words and phrases that were spoken.
- The app is also available in French and Spanish.
- $9.99

DAF Assistant
by ARTEFACT
http://www.artefactsoft.com/iphonedaf.htm

- Apple app
- DAF Assistant implements delayed auditory feedback (DAF) and frequency-shifting auditory feedback (FAF) techniques that are known to provide a "chorus" effect to help people with stuttering to speak more fluently.
- The application provides delay range from 20 to 320 milliseconds with 10 millisecond increments. FAF shifts the pitch of your voice. The application provides pitch shift in the range from one-half octave down to one-half octave up.
- The app cannot work during a phone call on the iPhone.
- The user needs headphones with a remote and microphone or a Bluetooth headset.
- $9.99

Dragon Dictation
by Nuance
http://www.dragonmobileapps.com

- Apple app
- Users press a button and then dictate a sentence or two into the device. No training is required.
- Punctuation marks can be dictated and the app adapts to the user's voice over time to improve accuracy.
- The speech is processed online and the text is transcribed into the note.
- The text can then be sent to an e-mail or placed into a document or onto a social networking site such as Facebook or Twitter.
- The app requires the Internet.
- It offers multilingual support.
- Free

Dragon for E-Mail

by Nuance

http://www.dragonmobileapps.com/bb/dragonforemail.html

- BlackBerry App
- Users press a button and then dictate a sentence or two into the device.
- The speech is processed online and the text is transcribed onto the phone.
- The text can then be sent to an e-mail or placed into a document.
- Free

Expressionist

by AdastraSoft

http://itunes.apple.com/us/app/expressionist/id318022654?mt=8

- Apple app
- This app was designed to help users express themselves and imitate the expressions of others.
- There are more than 120 commonly used expressions that are divided into categories such as greetings, feelings, requests, and questions.
- It also includes 1,000 nouns and presents them in a cartoon format that combines an illustrated image with a high-quality photo.
- The app is customizable.
- $9.99

iCommunicate

by Grembe Inc.

http://www.grembe.com/home/icommunicate

- Apple app
- Users can create pictures, flashcards, storyboards, and visual schedules with audio.
- Storyboards can have different forms such as task completions with checkmarks or a sequence of events shown together.
- Users can add pictures from files, searching in Google images within the app or selecting from many that are included with the app.
- Speech can be recorded to correspond to pictures and storyboards in any language. Text to speech can be on or off. Users can tap on the screen five times to view options when the app is locked.
- $34.99 for iPhone and $49.99 for iPad

iPracticeVerbs
by Smarty Ears
http://www.smartyearsapps.com
- Apple app
- More than 120 verbs are depicted with high-quality images and text, and audio of words and phrases are selected by touching a button.
- Users flip through the images by shaking the device or sliding a finger along the screen.
- Data can be saved.
- $10.99

Learn to Talk
by iLearntoTalk
http://www.ilearn2talk.com
- Apple app
- The app enhances language development in 1–3-year-old children, but also can be used with older individuals.
- Words are written, spoken, and pictured on flashcards to build vocabulary and early word combinations.
- As children flip through the flashcards, they hear the words and phrases said aloud.
- This app was designed for parents to lead their child through the natural hierarchy of communicative intent, beginning with high impact words, expanding meaning by changing intonation of speech, adding vocabulary including nouns and verbs, and then developing early syntax and simple combinations of words.
- When the title of the card is touched, the word is spelled aloud.
- $1.99

Look2Learn
by MDR
http://www.look2learn.com
- Apple app
- The app allows individuals to work at their communicative level using photographs to express their wants and needs. ·
- It includes 80 preloaded photographs in six different categories or the individual can use personal photos.
- There are options to customize the app for different age or cognitive levels, including the ability to hide some photos, to reduce choices, to rename photos with a term that the user would more easily recognize, to create categories not included, to resize photos, and to utilize emotion cards in place of photos.

- Natural voices are used for voice output.
- $24.99

Martha Speaks Dog Party
by PBS Kids
http://pbskids.org/mobile/apps.html
- Apple app
- This app was designed to improve vocabulary.
- There are four games to play. Children are introduced to new vocabulary as they interact with Martha the dog by dressing her, feeding her, and playing "Martha Says."
- It includes adorable and motivating animations.
- $2.99

Mobile Articulation Probes
by Smarty Ears
http://smartyearsapps.com
- Apple app
- This app was designed to help children improve articulation during speech therapy.
- There are 936 images in the phonemes menu with 2,700 images in all.
- Practice can be initiated by choosing phonemes (all 23 are available), mode of articulation (e.g., fricatives, glides, stops, liquids, affricates, nasals, and plosives), and phonological processes (e.g., fronting, backing, stopping, final consonant deletion, initial consonant deletion, gliding, and consonant cluster reduction).
- User performance can be tracked and homework with selected words can be e-mailed at the end of a session.
- A Spanish version is also available.
- $24.99

My Pictures Talk
by Grembe Inc.
http://www.grembe.com
- Apple app
- Users record utterances that are then added to pictures while in the editing mode.
- When viewing a picture, tap on it to play audio.
- Pictures can be sorted into categories.
- $4.99

MyTalkTools Mobile
by 2nd Half Enterprises
http://www.mytalktools.com

- Apple app
- This is an augmentative communication tool.
- Designed for maximum flexibilty, you can add images and audio by setting up grids and sequences directly via the mobile device or via Workspace, a web-based online authoring and content management system.
- The app includes more than 1,000 commonly used images and sounds that are available in a searchable library.
- The screen can be displayed on an external monitor.
- Text to speech can be accessed in the user mode.
- $39.99

NeoPaul and NeoKate
by NeoSpeech
http://www.neospeech.com

- Apple app
- Users enter any text and hear it spoken aloud in a very natural-sounding voice.
- Typed phrases and sentences can be saved.
- Free

Proloquo2Go
by AssistiveWare
http://www.proloquo2go.com

- Apple app
- Proloquo2Go is a fully featured augmentative communication system with an initial vocabulary of more than 7,000 items and the ability of users to form novel utterances with the dynamic display setup. The device says aloud the message selected or created by the user.
- The program is very flexible—users can configure the size and number of images on the screen, the organization of pages and items on the page, and the rate and type of voice used.
- Automorphology features enhance learning with the correct usage of verb tenses, possession, and plurals.
- Users can quickly access recently spoken items.
- There is a typing view for users who want to type and have the app read the text aloud.

- Branching support is provided to improve communication and increase the length of utterance.
- $189.99

Pronunciation Power
by English Computerized Learning
http://www.englishlearning.com/iphone

- Apple app
- It provides a visual display of how to pronounce all English sounds.
- Free (for a limited time)

/r/ intensive
by Smarty Ears
http://www.smartyearsapps.com

- This app is geared toward use by a speech-language pathologist to remediate the /r/ sound.
- It uses a phonetic approach to teaching the /r/ sound with sub-groups to enhance success such as prevocalic r, /ar/ and /er/.
- There is a probe option to help the therapist know which /r/ to work on.
- Both word and phrase levels are available. More than 450 target words are included.
- Percentage accuracy can be tallied and saved.
- $17.99

Sentence Builder
by Mobile Education Tools
http://www.mobile-educationstore.com

- Apple app
- This app was designed to help users learn how to build grammatically correct sentences.
- Emphasis is placed on the usage of connector words that make up a large part of the English language.
- Users rotate words on a wheel to form a sentence that matches pictures. For each picture, there is only one correct combination of words.
- In the easiest level, the subject and the adjective are fixed and the user needs to select the modifier and verb. In Levels 2 and 3, more words need to be selected.
- Verbal expression can be improved by having the individual read the sentence aloud.

- Progress is recorded for each level.
- $3.99

SmallTalk Aphasia
by Lingraphica
http://aphasia.com

- Apple app
- This app comes with a starter set of icons and videos that are most appropriate for adults. It was developed to help people with aphasia communicate.
- Preloaded icons appear in a list with text that the user can press and have said aloud to engage in conversation.
- A set of videos is included that show up-close lip movement for words and functional phrases for practice and self-cueing.
- This app is meant to be used as an accessory to the Lingraphica—a customizable speech generating device for people with aphasia available at http://www.aphasia.com.
- Free

SpeakinMotion Trial
by SpeakinMotion
http://www.speakinmotion.com

- Apple app
- This app provides personalized, up-close video content of four different mouth models that can be used online, on a mobile device, or on a DVD to practice speech.
- It was produced to help adults with apraxia, but is helpful for many other people who have difficulty speaking.
- Prerecorded scripts can be used for everyday life communication.
- The functional section includes scripts for conversation, telephone calls, dining, public speaking, jokes, literature, and religion.
- The therapy section includes up-close videos to practice utterances such as months, compound words, and rhyming words.
- An emergency section and videos to help users get started are integrated into the app.
- It is suggested that rather than repeat the verbalizations, the users should practice with the benefit of simultaneous visual, auditory, and sometimes written cues during verbal production attempts.
- This trial app is free, but in order to personalize scripts a subscription is needed.

Speak it!
by Future Apps
http://www.future-apps.net

- Apple app
- Users type text and the application highlights the words as they are read aloud in a clear natural-sounding voice.
- Additional voices in different languages are available.
- Messages can be saved for later use and sent to others as a sound file as well as searched through for target words.
- $1.99

Story Builder
by Mobile Education Tools
http://www.mobile-educationstore.com

- Apple app
- This app uses a series of questions and text prompts to help the user answer the questions verbally. The responses to the questions provide the storyline.
- There are 50 storylines to create narratives and more than 500 audio clips of questions to guide the utterances.
- The easiest level of play uses a series of questions and text prompts to help the user answer questions verbally. The responses to the questions provide the storyline.
- The harder levels are more open-ended in the story creation.
- The recordings can be used to focus on articulation and fluency as well as content.
- This app presents three levels of play to record narratives.
- $3.99

Talk Assist
by Mubaloo
http://itunes.apple.com/us/app/talk-assist/id329338159?mt=8

- Apple app
- Users can create and have the device speak sentences as well as keep a history and bookmark particular phrases for convenience.
- Free

TouchChat

by Silver Kite

http://www.silver-kite.com

- Apple app
- A fully featured, customizable augmentative communication app that enables users to communicate words and phrases as well as longer messages by selecting pictures and text.
- Five voices and more than 10,000 symbols are included.
- A unique feature for noisy environments is the ability of the user to tilt the device and have the message expand to fill the entire screen for others to read.
- Four page sets are included: one for adults and adolescents with developmental disabilities, another for school-age children with emerging language skills, a third for individuals who want to type with word prediction buttons and prestored phrases, and a fourth for young children who need vocabulary for home, school, and general communication.
- Additional page sets are available for purchase or can be downloaded with a subscription to iShare.
- $149.99

WhQuestions

by Smarty Ears

http://www.smartyearsapps.com

- Apple app
- This app was developed to help children answer questions involving who, what, where, how, and why.
- The app provides 300 questions in a variety of formats that can be customized.
- Questions are provided in a written format and audio options are available to ask the questions aloud.
- A helper indicates if verbal responses are correct or incorrect.
- Users respond by tapping on the appropriate picture or verbalizing the response.
- Users slide a finger across the screen to proceed to the next question.
- Scores are saved to show progress.
- $9.99

CHAPTER 5

ADDITIONAL TOOLS AND RESOURCES TO HELP IMPROVE VERBAL EXPRESSION

There are many tools and resources that can be used to help improve verbal expression in addition to the wide variety of software and apps presented in the last chapter. Augmentative and Alternative Communication (AAC) focuses on helping individuals whose speech does not meet their communication needs. Consistency with treatment and training on the use of these tools is the key to the successful integration of them into a person's daily life. Family and close friends as well as teachers and colleagues need to be part of this process and learn how best to facilitate functional conversations with persons using these assistive therapy tools.

There are many types of devices and assistive communication tools and strategies that can be used to facilitate expressive communication, including:

✓ simple communication items without voice output;
✓ dedicated communication devices;
✓ direct-select, one-level, voice output communication devices;
✓ multiple-level, voice output devices;
✓ dynamic display, voice output devices;
✓ communication software that can be used on the client's computer;
✓ devices and software that use a client's own speech to clarify the message; and
✓ telephones and videophones.

SIMPLE COMMUNICATION ITEMS WITHOUT VOICE OUTPUT

Symbols, pictures, and words can be used to facilitate communication. Books, picture communication charts, calendars, maps, and other items may be able to help augment expressive communication. Many of these products can be purchased in multiple languages. The term *symbols* in AAC refers to both unaided and aided symbols. Unaided symbols include gestures, facial expressions, sign language, and body posture. Aided symbols include objects, photographs, line drawings, picture communication symbols, and the alphabet. These simple communication items are often most effective when they are personalized. In addition to being used to augment communication, they can be used to practice new verbal skills. For more information, check out the products at the following websites:

- ✓ **AliMed**: http://www.alimed.com
  - ▶ Communicard Trio
  - ▶ The Critical Communicator
  - ▶ The Critical Communicator for Kids
  - ▶ Daily Communicator
  - ▶ VisiBoard Picture Communication Board

- ✓ **Logan ProxTalker**: http://www.proxtalker.com
- ✓ **Picture Dictionaries**: http://amazon.com and http://barnesandnoble.com
  - ▶ *The Oxford Picture Dictionary: Monolingual English Edition*
  - ▶ *The Oxford Picture Dictionary for the Content Areas—Monolingual English Edition*

- ✓ **Topic Boards**: http://www.communication-innovations.com
- ✓ **Vidatak EZ Board**: http://www.vidatak.com

DEDICATED COMMUNICATION DEVICES

Many devices are available to assist users in the selection of multiple icons or words to convey complex ideas and concepts. There is a lot to keep in mind during the selection process such as:

- ✓ the user's level of acceptance,
- ✓ characteristics of the communication partners,
- ✓ the environment in which communication will take place,
- ✓ the features of the strategies and systems, and
- ✓ the capabilities and challenges of the individual.

New devices are now combining the capabilities of speech-generating devices with Internet access and features of consumer electronics, such as iPods, cameras, and cell phones.

Tips for Selecting a Communication Device

- ◆ It's important to decide the best way to represent language on the selected system: pictures, symbols, or words. Some people with severe verbal apraxia have intact language skills and are able to use text to communicate. Those with severely delayed language or aphasia typically are only able to use pictures and probably will need help learning to sequence pictures to convey complex thoughts.

- ◆ You'll need to make judgments about visual displays, sound output, and the method of selection.

- ◆ Consider the social network of the user, the environment, and the purposes for which the device will be used. A person with expressive communication deficits will communicate differently with family, close friends, paid caregivers, teachers, acquaintances, and strangers. There is much more to communication than just labeling objects.

- ◆ Use expensive devices on a trial basis prior to purchase. Each state has an assistive technology program (see http://www.resnaprojects. org/nattap/at/statecontacts.html), and many of these offer equipment loans at no cost. Many manufacturers rent their devices for trial use.

- ◆ Listen to the voice on the device. The Microsoft voices and DECtalk synthesizers are more robotic-sounding than the AT&T, Acapela, and NeoSpeech voices. More natural sounding voices can be purchased at http://www.nextup.com. They provide samples of the voices on the website. The voice files cost $25–$60. It is important to make sure the computer or device you want to use is compatible with the purchased voice.

PEOPLE WHO CAN BENEFIT FROM AUGMENTATIVE COMMUNICATION DEVICES

Detailed information about all of the devices on the market and their features is beyond the scope of this book. Many informative books and helpful websites are available, including, but not limited to the following:

- ✓ *Augmentative and Alternative Communication for Adults With Acquired Neurologic Disorders*, edited by David R. Beukelman, Kathryn M. Yorkston, and Joe Reichle
- ✓ *Augmentative and Alternative Communication: Supporting Children and Adults With Complex Communication Needs* (3rd ed.), by David R. Beukelman and Pat Mirenda
- ✓ **AAC Institute**: http://www.aacinstitute.org
- ✓ **AAC TechConnect**: http://www.aacpartners.com
- ✓ **Alliance for Technology Access**: http://www.ataccess.org
- ✓ **Closing the Gap**: http://www.closingthegap.com
- ✓ **Rehabtool.com**: http://www.rehabtool.com
- ✓ **United States Society for Augmentative and Alternative Communication**: http://www.ussaac.org

DIRECT-SELECT, ONE-LEVEL, VOICE OUTPUT COMMUNICATION DEVICES

Direct-select, one-level, voice output communication devices are relatively simple devices where messages are created on the device or are already programmed and activated by pressing a button to select a picture, word, or phrase. These communication devices include everything from talking picture frames and talking photo albums to more specialized tools. Numerous alternatives are available from http://www.ablenetinc.com, http://EnablingDevices.com, and http://Mayer-Johnson.com.

Direct-select, one-level, talking communication devices can be used as a stepping stone to determine readiness for more complex devices. These talking devices use pictures and words that the person who programs the device determines are most important for the individual to communicate. When the user selects the picture, a prerecorded word or phrase is played aloud on the device. By selecting a picture or word, users may be able to "verbalize" their basic needs and wants in real life and practice the utterances in therapy. If the user is unable to initiate use of these tools, the devices are often helpful for the communication partner. The combination of the picture and voice output helps comprehension. These talking devices are also helpful when a person is unable to rely on nonverbal communication (writing, gesturing, or drawing) for long-distance communication.

Software and apps in this category that turn computers, iPhones, iPod touches, and iPads into direct-select, one-level, talking communication devices were highlighted in Chapter 4.

* *

GoTalk

by Attainment Company

http://www.attainmentcompany.com

- Several versions are available, with varying numbers of pictures.
- Multiple layers of pictures can be recorded.
- The price range is from $12.00 for GoTalk One to $599.00 for GoTalk Express 32.

Listen to Me

by DTK Enterprises

http://www.listentome.biz

- This one-level communication device is accessed by pressing the keys on the front.
- The 12 keys have sleeves that allow graphics to be inserted onto the faces.
- $79.00

Livescribe Echo Pen

by Livescribe

http://www.livescribe.com

- This pen records all that is said as the user writes. The recorded audio can be replayed by tapping directly on the special dot paper with the pen that recorded the audio.
- MyScript from Livescribe provides handwriting recognition so that the text can be converted to a Word document.
- Notes can be saved and searched for online or on a computer.
- Apps are available for games, reference guides, and productivity tools.
- Notes and recordings can be shared using the Pencast application. These recordings can be sent with an e-mail or embedded online.
- Creative users can use this pen to make talking flashcards, schedules, communication boards, and memory books by recording speech on the special paper and then cutting up the paper and putting the pieces on index cards or in a scrapbook.
- 4 GB Echo Smartpen: $169.95 for 400 hours of audio (varies by audio quality setting)

Talking Photo Albums
http://www.augcominc.com/index.cfm/talking_photo_album.htm
- Talking photo albums enable the user to press a section on the bottom of an album page and hear spoken words corresponding to a picture made by the person who programmed it.
- The recordings can be of single words naming the picture or phrases describing the photo.
- $29.00

The AAC Idea Book: Creative Ways to Use Talking Photo Albums
by Sarah W. Blackstone and Harvey Pressman
http://www.augcominc.com/index.cfm/talking_photo_album.htm
- This book contains 21 ideas contributed by 14 AAC experts regarding the many ways to use a talking photo album in therapy.
- You can use the talking photo album to give instructions, tell stories, record autobiographical information, facilitate daily conversation, help order in restaurants, and facilitate memory.
- $18.00

Pictures That Talk: New Ways to Use Talking Photo Albums
by Juli Trautman Pearson and Harvey Pressman
http://www.augcominc.com/index.cfm/talking_photo_album.htm
- This book offers suggestions for using pictures, text, and recorded messages to improve communication skills and foster independence.
- $29.00

DYNAMIC COMMUNICATION DEVICES, APPS, AND SOFTWARE

Devices with dynamic display capabilities automatically change the picture displays and corresponding messages using internal hyperlinks. Novel messages can be communicated through sequential selection of pictures or words. Some of the devices are on tablet PCs with a touch screen, some work on smaller handheld devices, and some are on notebook computers. Dynamic display software is also now available online, as well as on devices such as the iPod touch, the iPad, and smartphones.

Dynamic communication devices use either digitized or synthesized speech and are specifically designed to replace or augment speech. Digitized communication devices use recorded speech for the messages that will be heard by the communicators. Synthesized communication devices translate text into electronic speech. Medicare and other reimbursement services may pay for them given sufficient documentation if the devices are only used for communication purposes.

A comprehensive review of these devices is beyond the scope of this book. Software and apps were highlighted in Chapter 4. Please refer to the following websites for additional information:

- ✓ **DynaVox**: http://www.dynavoxtech.com
- ✓ **Gus Communication Devices**: http://www.gusinc.com
- ✓ **Lingraphica**: http://www.aphasia.com
- ✓ **4StrokeSurvivors.com**: http://www.4strokesurvivors.com
- ✓ **PRC**: http://www.prentrom.com
- ✓ **Saltillo**: http://www.saltillo.com
- ✓ **Words+**: http://www.words-plus.com
- ✓ **ZYGO Industries**: http://www.zygo-usa.com

Several companies offer software that users can install on their own computers to turn them into communication devices. There is controversy in the professional world about this approach. On the positive side, users can then save the expense of purchasing another computer on which the dedicated communication devices are produced. When users purchase the communication software, they can use the computer they have with other software and features, such as Internet access and the use of word processing programs. A negative view is that the computer might not offer features that are needed for functional communication devices, such as "instant on" features, high-quality speakers, durability, and long battery life. Text-to-speech software, which is discussed later in this book, is also a great tool to use to augment communication.

DEVICES AND SOFTWARE USING A PERSON'S OWN SPEECH TO CLARIFY THE MESSAGE

Several devices and software programs make residual verbal expression abilities more functional. Voice amplifiers and a product that clarifies the speech called the Voice Enhancer are helpful for people with Parkinson's, multiple sclerosis, and other conditions that cause a strain on the larynx. They also are helpful for professionals who place heavy demands on their voices such as teachers, trainers, and presenters. Individuals with benign lesions such as nodules resulting from vocal abuse (yelling, screaming, loud talking, or excessive singing) can also benefit from amplifiers and clarifiers. The devices offer hands-free communication and are lightweight. They can be worn on a belt, in a pocket, or around the neck. Medicare covers amplifiers for some people.

* *

ChatterVox
by ChatterVox
http://www.chattervox.com
- This voice amplification system gives 15 decibels of voice boost.
- It is a lightweight unit that is designed to be worn at the waist.
- There are both over-the-ear and collar-style microphones. Both have an adjustable boom, so that the microphone can be positioned very close to the mouth for the best amplification with the least vocal effort.
- $260.00

Speech Enhancer SGD
by Voicewave Technology
http://www.speechenhancer.com
- This device makes speech clearer, restores an inaudible voice, and boosts computer speech-recognition accuracy.
- Each system has a microphone and a lightweight voice-processing unit that is worn at the waist or mounted on a wheelchair.
- Various models offer telephone and wireless capabilities and support for computer speech-recognition software.
- It is available only through an evaluation by an independent certified evaluator who provides the pricing information.

Voice Saver
by Califone
http://www.hearmore.com
- Two-watt amplifier with separate tone and volume controls.
- Plug in the microphone, clip it to your belt, and turn it on.
- It weighs less than a pound and comes complete with a headset microphone, four AA rechargeable batteries, a charging adaptor, and an adjustable belt.
- $119.95

SentenceShaper 2
by Psycholinguistic Technologies
http://www.bungalowsoftware.com

- This program helps people with significant aphasia and verbal apraxia by recording parts of intelligible speech and allowing the user to produce narratives by selecting them to communicate messages.
- The purpose is to facilitate spoken language by serving as a "processing prosthesis." It allows users to record spoken fragments and assemble them into sentences by manipulating icons on a computer screen.
- SentenceShaper 2 comes with 15 built-in therapy workbooks (approximately 800 pages in all). Each therapy workbook contains a set of pages designed to help the user practice a particular grammatical structure, using colorful pictures and providing spoken prompts, models of the target sentence, and word-finding help for each picture. The structures trained include simple sentences (subject, verb, direct object), prepositional phrases, adjectives, and subordinate clauses with *because* and *while*.
- Windows
- $399.50 for the home version; $649.50 for the Pro+editing version

The following sites provide additional products and information:
- ✓ **Luminaud**: http://www.luminaud.com
- ✓ **RadioShack**: http://www.radioshack.com
- ✓ **Saltillo**: http://www.saltillo.com
- ✓ **Professional Speech Aid Service**: http://www.speechaid.com
- ✓ **Communicative Medical**: http://www.communicativemedical.com
- ✓ **SoundBytes**: http://www.soundbytes.com

EMERGENCY ALERTS, TELEPHONES, VIDEOPHONES, AND ASSISTIVE OPTIONS

EMERGENCY ALERTS/PERSONAL EMERGENCY RESPONSE SYSTEM (PERS)

For people who are alone and who have difficulty with expressive communication, a subscription to a medical alert service or personal emergency response system that is connected to a local hospital can be helpful. For more information, go to one of the following websites or try searching on a search engine such as Google with the key words "senior emergency alerts." Another suggestion is to talk to your physician or medical supply center or even a pharmacist. Your social service department at the hospital may help.

✓ **Philips Lifeline**: http://www.lifelinesystems.com
✓ **MedicAlert Foundation**: http://www.medicalert.com

TELEPHONES

The telephone is one of the main tools of our everyday lives. It is an important means of communicating in emergencies, accessing information, and maintaining contact with family and friends. However, it is difficult to use for people with verbal expression issues. Without its benefits, depression and feelings of isolation can become problematic and hinder the learning and rehabilitation process. We can help people compensate for phone-related challenges in many ways. One of those is relay service access.

✓ A telecommunications relay service is provided free of charge to anyone who needs communication assistance. For more information about this, contact http://www.fcc.gov/cgb/dro/trs.html.

✓ Speech-to-speech (STS) service is for a person with a speech disability. The individual talks (or uses her communication device to convey her message) to a communications assistant with special training in listening and understanding a variety of speech disorders. The communications assistant repeats everything, making the caller's words clear and understandable, and then makes the call for that person.

✓ In hearing carryover (HCO)—so called because the person with the speech disability can hear the other party's voice—people who have difficulty speaking on the phone can place or receive calls by typing what they want to say using a special telephone called a text telephone (TTY). A communications assistant then reads the caller's words to the person receiving the call. Three-way calling is necessary for an HCO call.

The FCC has reserved 711 for relay service access. Just as 411 can be called for information, 711 can be dialed to connect to relay service anywhere in the United States.

CELL PHONES

Cell phones have become increasingly important in today's society. Pay phones are rare and often do not function. People with difficulty communicating should carry a cell phone if they travel alone in the community, so that they can call others who are familiar with their situation for help as needed. If they are unable to talk, the caller ID can signal to the recipient of the call who they are and that person can bear the conversational burden by asking yes/no questions or other helpful communication techniques.

For individuals who have relatively preserved cognitive abilities, sequencing skills, and manual dexterity, features of smartphones can augment communication abilities. Phones now come equipped with cameras, text messaging, voice recognition, apps, and more. With a bit of imagination and creativity, these devices can become powerful communication assistants. The following useful features provide examples:

✓ **Address book**: Helpful for recalling names of people.

✓ **Calendar**: Helpful for remembering and organizing and for referring to names, dates, and places in conversation.

✓ **Still and video cameras**: Provide an effective way to communicate by sending a person a picture of a situation, a person, a place, or an event.

✓ **Apps**: Offer text-to-speech and communication assistance. Many apps that work for the iPhone were reviewed in the last chapter. Android phones are also becoming increasingly popular.

ACCESSIBLE CELL PHONES

People with physical, communication, or cognitive disabilities frequently find the use of a standard handset with small buttons difficult to use. The following websites may help you find the appropriate type of phone:

✓ **Firefly Mobile**: http://www.fireflymobile.com

✓ **ETOEngineering.com**: http://www.etoengineering.com

✓ **Just5 Simple Features**: http://www.just5.com

✓ **SightConnection**: http://www.sightconnection.com

ADAPTED LANDLINE PHONES

Large buttons, preprogrammed numbers, pictures for preprogrammed locations or people, and integrated answering machines are helpful phone features for people with challenges. For more information, check out these sites:

✓ **EnableMart**: http://www.enablemart.com

✓ **101Phones.com**: http://www.101phones.com

✓ **Hearmore.com**: http://www.hearmore.com

VIDEOPHONES

Telephones that can transmit and receive both video and audio signals, allowing people to see as well as hear each other, are called videophones. They have become much more affordable and make long-distance communication easier. Some videophones resemble regular phones with the use of video.

✓ Face-to-face contact is very helpful for people with communication deficits. The use of gestures, facial expressions, contextual cues, calendars, writing, and communication devices to augment verbal utterances helps with the effectiveness of the interaction. Being able to see the person you are talking to is a big advantage.

✓ Videocalls can be made on telephones and other handheld devices. Cell phones that play video are becoming increasingly popular. Almost all of the major carriers now have 3G and 4G networks that let you to stream video with increasing speed to your phone through a wireless broadband connection.

✓ The most recent iPhone and Android phones are now able to be used as videophones (callers can see each other as they speak) when certain apps are used. The Android app called fring and the Apple app called FaceTime can turn these phones into videophones under a set of conditions.

✓ There are also videophones that are Internet-based and require the use of a computer with a webcam. The ability to talk over the computer uses Voice Over Internet Protocol (VOIP). An example is Skype at http://www.skype.com. Skype is a program for making free calls over the Internet to anyone who also has Skype. It's free and easy to download and use, it works with most computers, and there are apps for use on the iPhone and iPad. Webcams on either end enable the speakers to see the other party. The calls have excellent sound quality and are highly secure, with end-to-end encryption.

For several options, go to these websites:
✓ **Wind Currents Technology**: http://www.videophoneconnection.com
✓ **Apple**: http://www.apple.com
✓ **Verizon Wireless**: http://www.verizonwireless.com
✓ **Google voice and video chat**: http://www.google.com/chat/video

VIDEOCONFERENCING

A videoconference is a set of interactive telecommunication technologies that allows two or more locations to interact via two-way video and audio transmissions at the same time. For people with communication and cognitive challenges, video conferencing is a great way to communicate because nonverbal communication can augment verbal messages.

Skype

http://www.skype.com

- Voice and video calls to anyone else on Skype are free.
- Conference calls with three or more people are available.
- Instant messaging, file transfer, and screen sharing are available.
- Free

ooVoo

http://www.oovoo.com

- Free two-way video chats.
- Users can use text chat and send files.
- Premium accounts are available.
- Free

CHAPTER 6

TECHNOLOGY TO IMPROVE AUDITORY COMPREHENSION

It is devastating when a person is unable to understand spoken language. Listening and understanding play a crucial role in our daily lives. In conversation, we translate speech into meaningful language. As we listen, we decode and identify meaningful words effortlessly. In many ways, computers and technology can help children and adults who have a hard time understanding what is said to them. Computers can both compensate for and provide drill and practice for activities to improve the comprehension of words, directions, and conversations. Computer use empowers individuals with auditory challenges to increase the time spent practicing skills taught by the communication and cognitive specialist.

In this chapter, assistive technologies are highlighted that can be used to enhance auditory comprehension. As with verbal expression, a multimedia approach using sound, text, and pictures helps with understanding.

People with auditory comprehension and processing deficits may have the following characteristics:

✓ demonstrate a short attention span,
✓ show signs of distractibility,
✓ display an oversensitivity to sounds,
✓ misinterpret what is said to them,
✓ confuse words,
✓ need frequent repetition,
✓ are unable to follow directions,
✓ have difficulty with speech and verbal expression, and
✓ show poor reading comprehension.

In children, a central auditory processing disorder (CAPD) occurs when the ear and the brain do not coordinate fully. Auditory information breaks down somewhere beyond the ear. Because the majority of early learning is auditory, a weakness in how language is processed can lead to delayed development with reading. Auditory processing is a critical component to reading success.

In adults, language-based, auditory comprehension deficits are referred to as *receptive aphasia*. The causes are varied, and they can include head trauma and stroke.

As with other language modalities, working to improve auditory comprehension is a complex task. The reasons for the difficulty need to be thoroughly evaluated, so that the strategies and practice are appropriate. A person may appear not to understand, but the problem may be complicated by a variety of other issues, such as problems with hearing, processing, and memory. Prior to the selection of products, it's essential to analyze the major obstacles of comprehension and figure out what is needed to improve it. Professional help should be used whenever possible.

TREATMENT APPROACH

As reiterated throughout this book, it is best not to use computerized programs exclusively to improve deficits, because everyone needs one-on-one feedback and modeling from peers, siblings, parents, therapists, and teachers. However, computer programs often enhance the progress.

When assisting people who have difficulty understanding what is said to them, it is helpful to find other ways to enhance the message being said, such as the following:

✓ Show communication partners how to use the environment to support the message. The use of gestures, pictures, written words, calendars, clocks, objects, and actions should be used.

✓ Speak more slowly, face the listener, and articulate speech well.

✓ Minimize external distractions such as the TV and other extraneous visual and auditory stimuli.

✓ Provide multisensory cues. People do best when they can see a word, hear a word, and perhaps touch an object.

✓ Present words in their natural context. For instance, try to talk about food items while in the kitchen, or have a calendar to refer to while talking about dates.

✓ Engage in activities that help people become more aware of the sounds around them, listen for patterns of sounds, discriminate differences between sounds, and become more observant of letter sounds (phonemes).

Computer Software to Help Improve Auditory Comprehension

Different software programs provide different ways of assisting with or compensating for auditory comprehension challenges. Many of the apps listed in the verbal expression and reading comprehension chapters of this book can also be used to help improve auditory comprehension.

Brain Fitness Program
by Posit Science
http://positscience.com

- This program was designed to sharpen the brain's auditory system using a series of carefully controlled listening tasks to improve the brain's ability to receive, interpret, and store auditory information.
- Multiple exercises are provided that target different cognitive functions such as sound processing when presented quickly, distinguishing between similar sounds, remembering the order of sounds, and improving working and short-term memory.
- The program gets harder and easier automatically in response to the user's performance.
- Data are collected to document progress.
- Users are encouraged to practice daily.
- $395.00

BrainPro and BrainSpark
by Scientific Learning
http://www.brainsparklearning.com

- Theses programs are designed for students and use exercises from the Fast ForWord family of products to improve sequencing, processing rate, attention, recall and memory, and knowledge.
- BrainPro was developed for struggling students and uses tutors to monitor the users' progress and provide guidance to parents or teachers.
- BrainSpark was developed for children who are reading at or above grade level.
- Windows and Mac
- Contact providers on the website for pricing.

Direction Following +Out Loud
by Bungalow Software
http://www.bungalowsoftware.com

- The user hears and/or reads directions and follows them by moving shapes on the screen with the mouse or keyboard.
- $139.50 for a single home user
- $50.00 as part of a monthly subscription.

Earobics
by Cognitive Concepts
http://www.donjohnston.com and http://www.enablemart.com

- There are two versions, each of which offers hundreds of levels of instruction.
- Each level is specially developed to help students build critical literacy skills, including recognizing and blending sounds, rhyming, and discriminating phonemes within words.
- Windows and Mac
- $65.00 (home version)

Fast ForWord
by Scientific Learning
http://www.scilearn.com

- There are a number of research-supported programs available that families can access via trained providers.
- The software focuses on developing and strengthening memory, attention, processing rate, and sequencing.
- Contact the company for pricing and providers.

Following Directions Series
by Laureate Learning Systems
http://www.laureatefamily.com

- This program offers many different activities that teach one-level, sequential, and two-level commands using spatial relations and directional terms.
- Windows and Mac
- $87.50 for One and Two-Level Command for family edition

Hear Builder: Following Directions
by Super Duper Inc
http://www.hearbuilder.com

- HearBuilder is a series of educational software programs designed to help students improve their listening skills.

- This evidence-based, interactive software program is designed to help all children, particularly those with autism, learn how to follow directions as they learn 40 basic concepts.
- These concepts are in five primary areas: basic directions, sequential directions, quantitative and spatial directions, temporal directions, and conditional directions.
- Windows and Mac
- $69.95 for the home edition

Hoop Nut
by Scientific Learning
http://www.scilearn.com/products/brainapps/hoop-nut

- Hoop Nut is an online exercise that will test your auditory processing speed and ability to focus attention. Click the yellow acorn on the tree launcher and you will hear a target syllable first. Listen carefully as the two "astro-nuts" in the acorns each present a syllable. Click the astro-nut that presents the target syllable.
- Free

Lunar Tunes
by Scientific Learning
http://www.scilearn.com/products/brainapps/lunar-tunes

- Lunar Tunes is an online exercise that will test auditory and visual-spatial memory.
- An amplifier with a grid of speakers is displayed and each speaker has a syllable or word associated with it. The user clicks a speaker to hear a syllable or word pronounced. Individuals then click the other speakers on the amplifier to find the speaker with the matching syllable or word.
- Free

My House, My Town, and My School:
The Language Activities of Daily Living Series
by Laureate Learning Systems
http://www.laureatelearning.com

- There are six scenes in each program with customizable options.
- There are tasks asking the user to select items based on their names or functions.
- Windows and Mac
- $195.00 for each edition

No-Glamour Auditory Processing Interactive Software
by Carolyn LoGiudice
http://www.linguisystems.com

- This product is an auditory perceptual training program designed for use by children with learning or communication disabilities.
- The activities range from simple, auditory reception skills to complex, problem-solving tasks.
- The program improves auditory processing skills in the areas of: auditory reception, following directions, recognizing absurdities, phonological awareness, details, exclusion, identifying the main idea, problem solving, riddles, and comprehension.
- The program can be used by an unlimited number of users.
- Lessons can be customized for each student.
- Pre- and posttest results, session responses, and student progress can be recorded and documented.
- Windows and Mac
- $43.95

SoundSmart
by BrainTrain
http://www.braintrain.com

- This software was designed to improve listening skills, ability to follow directions, phonemic awareness, working memory, mental processing speed, and impulse control.
- It includes a set of 11 multilevel talking Bingo games.
- SoundSmart consists of three modules: Attention Coach, Math and Memory Coach, and Sound Discrimination Coach. Users can access thousands of tasks within each program and customize them for an individual's needs.
- Contact BrainTrain for pricing options.

Spotlight on Reading & Listening Comprehension Interactive Software
by Linda Bowers, Rosemary Huisingh, Carolyn LoGuidice,
Paul F. Johnson, and Jane Orman
http://www.linguisystems.com

- This software includes more than 60 narrated stories and 480 multiple-choice questions.
- There are several reading levels.
- Students listen to and read aloud each story and its follow-up questions and answers.

- Narrated audio can be turned on and off at any time.
- Each story screen includes a full-color picture to help visual learners attach meaning to the text. Users can review the text of the story as they answer comprehension questions.
- $59.95

The Listening Program
by Advanced Brain Technologies
http://www.advancedbrain.com
- The Listening Program is a music-based auditory stimulation method that trains the brain to improve the auditory skills needed to listen, learn, and communicate.
- The program consists of 15–30 minutes a day of music specifically recorded for this purpose.
- Providers are listed on the website.

Understanding Questions +Out Loud
by Bungalow Software
http://www.bungalowsoftware.com
- This program provides practice with understanding various types of questions including: Who? What? When? Where? Why? and How?
- The type and number of questions asked can be tailored to the needs of the user. Information can be presented auditorily as well as visually.
- Windows
- $139.50 (Home edition)

Long-Distance Communication

Communicating on the phone is difficult if someone has a hard time with auditory comprehension. Several solutions are available.

TELEPHONES
Special landlines, cell phones, videophones, and relay services can help people with auditory comprehension deficits communicate over a distance. Several of these were discussed in the last chapter.

TEXT
For a person who has difficulty understanding spoken language, text-based communication methods can augment comprehension. E-mailing,

faxing, and instant messaging may be more effective when a person is attempting to communicate with someone who is not in his or her immediate environment.

Google Voice
by Google
http://www.google.com/googlevoice/about.html
- Google offers a free innovative messaging service called Google Voice that includes a voice-to-text transcription feature that has strong possibilities to help people who struggle with auditory comprehension as well as English language learners.

ASSISTIVE LISTENING DEVICES

Assistive listening devices (ALDs) include a large variety of devices designed to improve comprehension in specific listening situations. Some are designed to be used with cochlear implants or hearing aids with a T-switch, while others are designed to be used alone. Assistive listening devices improve the listener's ability to hear by making the desired sound stand out from the background noise. Being able to hear can have a major impact on a person's ability to participate in social, academic, and work situations. Additional information can be found on these websites:

✓ **Advanced Affordable Hearing**: http://www.advancedhearing.com
✓ **Assistive Listening Device Systems**: http://www.alds.com
✓ **Harris Communications**: http://www.harriscomm.com
✓ **Hearing Loss Web**: http://www.hearinglossweb.com

CAPTIONING

CLOSED CAPTIONING

Closed captions contain text that is hidden within normal television broadcasts and on videotapes and DVDs. A television with the built-in caption decoder chip or an external decoder is needed to make the captions visible. It can typically be turned on or off by viewing the menu of options available on the TV. There's no special service to subscribe to in order to receive the captions. Captioning is made free for all viewers by the television and home video industries, with the support of grants and donations. This multisensory experience of watching captioned TV has been shown to significantly improve the reading skills of children. In addition, people learning English can improve their language and vocabulary skills, and adults with auditory comprehension deficits can improve their comprehension of the spoken material.

REAL-TIME CAPTIONING

Real-time captioning currently takes place when a person types what is said into a stenotype machine. The machine is connected to a computer with software that translates the shorthand into words in caption formats and standard spellings. It is now becoming possible to tape lectures and presentations, then to use voice-recognition software to transcribe what is said. As technology advances, this procedure has enormous potential for helping people with communication and cognitive deficits. However, the accuracy of voice recognition software with dictation is inconsistent. Free software for closed captioning may be found at http://ncam.wgbh.org/webaccess/magpie.

Described and Captioned Media Program
http://www.dcmp.org
- This is a library of more than 4,000 open-captioned titles (videos, CD-ROM, and DVD). Several hundred titles are also streamed on the website. The videos are designed for students who are blind, visually impaired, deaf, hard of hearing, or deaf blind.

More information about captioning is available at:
- ✓ **National Institute on Deafness and Other Communication Disorders**: http://www.nidcd.nih.gov/health/hearing/caption.asp
- ✓ **NCI**: http://www.ncicap.org/livecap.asp

CHAPTER 7

TECHNOLOGY TO IMPROVE READING COMPREHENSION

Millions of people of all ages have difficulty reading. The deficits may be developmental or acquired. Impaired reading ability can be the result of a learning disability, language delay, stroke, head injury, cognitive deficit, or visual and perceptual problems.

Reading is a complex task. To help people effectively who are having difficulty reading, you need to understand where the problems arise. Reading issues can stem from auditory perception difficulties, visual perception difficulties, or language processing difficulties. Deficits range in severity and the impact that they have on a person's life. Many people who are able to read may read slowly and have difficulty processing what they read. They may be able to understand the words in the text, but are unable to synthesize the information in order to find the main idea, identify implied information, paraphrase the content, locate desired information, or write about what they read. Some people have difficulty reading English because it's not their primary language.

According to Bright Solutions for Dyslexia (1998), dyslexia "is a neurologically-based, often familial, disorder which interferes with the acquisition and processing of language" (para. 3). Varying in degrees of severity, it is manifested by difficulties in receptive and expressive language (including phonological processing), reading, writing, spelling, handwriting, and sometimes in arithmetic. Although dyslexia is a lifelong impairment, individuals with dyslexia frequently respond successfully to timely and appropriate intervention. For more information about dyslexia, visit http://www.interdys.org/InsInt.htm.

Tools needed to improve and compensate for reading challenges of different etiologies vary. As with other communication and literacy challenges, specialists should be consulted whenever possible to maximize progress. Successful use of assistive devices and drill-and-practice software depends on:

- ✓ pairing the appropriate tools with the individual based on his or her deficits,
- ✓ training the individual to use the product or device, and
- ✓ providing appropriate support to resolve problems and help integrate new learning into everyday routines.

People who have difficulty with reading may present with many different scenarios. They may show the following difficulties:

- ✓ have overall poor literacy skills;
- ✓ be able to read aloud well, but show poor comprehension;
- ✓ understand the content, but are not able to remember it;
- ✓ go through the process of reading but when tested show little comprehension of what they appeared to read;
- ✓ get visually lost on the page or be unable to see the words;
- ✓ show slow processing time, which makes it difficult to keep up with reading demands at school or work, or may prevent reading for pleasure;
- ✓ demonstrate the ability to read basic information, but be unable to process complex material; and
- ✓ speak another language.

MULTIDISCIPLINARY APPROACH

Many professionals are able to assist in the treatment of reading challenges. Speech-language pathologists, occupational therapists, reading specialists, special education teachers, and vision specialists are trained to work on particular approaches to improve reading.

- ✓ Make sure that people with reading challenges who are suspected of having visually based deficits are evaluated and treated by an ophthalmologist or neuro-ophthalmologist.
- ✓ Research has shown that there is a close relationship between language development and literacy skills. Be sure to involve speech-language pathologists early whenever language development is delayed.
- ✓ The Individuals with Disabilities Education Act (http://idea.ed.gov) requires that school personnel, in conjunction with the child's

parents, develop an Individualized Education Program (IEP) for each student with learning disabilities who is eligible for special education.

✓ If the individual is returning to work, the Americans with Disabilities Act (ADA; http://www.usdoj.gov/crt/ada/adahom1.htm) requires that all employers provide reasonable accommodations for employees who are identified as having a disability.

There is quite a bit of research concerning the potential causes of reading difficulties and the most effective treatment options. It's been proven that people who have difficulty reading have a better chance of comprehending and retaining the content of written material with a guided reading approach and if they can simultaneously see the words and hear them read aloud.

Here are some helpful online resources:

✓ **ReadWriteThink**: http://www.readwritethink.org/parent-afterschool-resources

✓ **LD OnLine**: http://www.LDonline.org

✓ **National Institute of Child Health & Human Development**: http://www.nichd.nih.gov/crmc/cdb/reading.htm

✓ **National Center for Technology Innovation**: http://www.nationaltechcenter.org

✓ **TECHMATRIX**: http://www.techmatrix.org

ASSISTIVE READING TECHNOLOGY

Assistive reading technologies may help with the following:

✓ improving skills related to decoding, reading fluency, and comprehension by offering drill-and-practice exercises and reading the text aloud;

✓ transferring written material that is not in digital format into a format the computer can "read" using Optical Character Recognition (OCR), so that the text-to-speech software can read it aloud;

✓ using alternative book formats such as eBooks and talking books;

✓ improving strategies for synthesizing written information with the help of reading guides; and

✓ supporting reading, studying, writing, and electronic file management through the use of advanced, talking word processing software and online tools.

There are many treatment options to consider for both compensation and remediation of reading. In this chapter, the following topics are discussed:

✓ software and device features;
✓ computer accommodations for people with visual-perceptual deficits;
✓ assistive reading technology;
✓ text-to-speech capabilities;
✓ optical character recognition;
✓ free text readers;
✓ text readers with a few more features;
✓ advanced text readers with reading, writing, and studying tools;
✓ alternative book formats;
✓ online sites for audiobooks and eBooks;
✓ interactive talking books;
✓ adapted online newspapers;
✓ portable eBook readers; and
✓ handheld devices that read aloud.

SOFTWARE AND DEVICE FEATURES

During the software selection process, consider which of the following software features would be helpful for the person with the reading deficit:

✓ to focus on the development of improved auditory-perceptual skills and phonics to assist with reading;
✓ to pair text with graphics for users who can interpret pictures, but not the printed word;
✓ to provide written material and drill and practice with effective strategies to facilitate comprehension and analysis;
✓ to read aloud text that is printed on the computer screen, while also enlarging and highlighting the text;
✓ to change the format of the text to make it easier to view;
✓ to convert printed text from a paper or book into editable text to help with studying, to enable the material to be read aloud on a computer, or to be converted to WAV files for use in an MP3 or CD player;
✓ to work on visual tracking and scanning to improve reading fluency; and
✓ to give pronunciations aloud and definitions for words using portable spell checkers, translators, and reading pens.

COMPUTER ACCOMMODATIONS FOR PEOPLE WITH VISUAL-PERCEPTUAL DEFICITS

There are many options available for people with visual impairments that are already on many computers.

COMPUTERS WITH WINDOWS OPERATING SYSTEM

Computers that use a Windows operating system come with many built-in accessibility options. Users with low vision often depend on the ability to enlarge or enhance on-screen information. More detailed information can be found at http://www.microsoft.com/enable. To make on-screen information easier to see and to understand, use the display screens under the control panel on Windows-based computers.

- ✓ **Change the font style, color, and size of items on the desktop**: Using the display options, choose font color, size, and style combinations.
- ✓ **Change the icon size**: Make icons larger for visibility or smaller for increased screen space.
- ✓ **Alter screen resolution**: Change pixel count to enlarge objects on screen.
- ✓ **Provide high-contrast schemes**: Select color combinations that are easier to see.
- ✓ **Adjust cursor width and blink rate**: Make the cursor easier to locate or eliminate the distraction of its blinking.
- ✓ **Use a Microsoft Magnifier:** Enlarge portions of the screen for better visibility.
- ✓ **Use text-to-speech**: Narrator is a basic text-to-speech utility that reads what is displayed on the screen (i.e., the contents of the active window, menu options, or text that has been typed).

COMPUTERS WITH MAC OPERATING SYSTEM

There also are options built into Macintosh computers. Detailed information can be found at http://www.apple.com/accessibility. Solutions for people with visual impairments include the following options:

- ✓ **Zoom**: This feature includes a number of options, like the ability to set maximum and minimum values for rapid zooming in and out, a preview rectangle that outlines the portion of the screen that will be magnified, and the ability to customize how the screen moves as you navigate with the mouse pointer.

✓ **Change cursor size**: Mac OS X enables you to easily increase the size of the mouse cursor, so it's easier to find and follow when you move the mouse.

✓ **Use text-to-speech**: VoiceOver is a fully integrated, built-in screen reader technology that provides access to Apple computers through speech, audible cues, and keyboard navigation. Text-to-speech synthesis allows users to hear text read aloud. Simply select Speech from the Services menu of most applications, and hear the computer start speaking.

✓ **Increase the visual display**: View Options enables the user to increase icon size and text size for icons. Flexible display adjustments provide users with visually appealing options, such as a white-on-black display.

There are also quite a few programs on the market to assist people with low vision. It's beyond the scope of this guide to review them all. Additional information can be found on the following websites:

✓ **The Low Vision Gateway**: http://www.lowvision.org
✓ **EnableMart**: http://www.enablemart.com
✓ **Independent Living Aids**: http://www.independentliving.com

TEXT-TO-SPEECH

Software with text-to-speech capabilities can read aloud text on a computer screen. This multisensory input is very helpful for reading. It's visually engaging and increases reading speed, comprehension, and retention.

There are quite a few text-to-speech (TTS) products on the market. This software may include the following features:

✓ the ability to control auditory features and visual presentation;
✓ the ability to save the documents as auditory files that can be downloaded to handheld devices;
✓ options, such as voice, rate of speech, highlighting, and screen display, that can be individualized, depending on the software;
✓ text that can be read back a letter, word, line, sentence, or paragraph at a time;
✓ words that can be magnified as they are read aloud; and
✓ the ability to work with e-mail, websites, and Microsoft Word and PDF documents.

More sophisticated products with TTS can also:
- ✓ electronically highlight sections of text in different colors,
- ✓ take notes by typing or by voice,
- ✓ prepare outlines,
- ✓ create flashcards and other study materials,
- ✓ use word prediction,
- ✓ read only highlighted sections, and
- ✓ skip to the bookmarked section of text.

OPTICAL CHARACTER RECOGNITION

Optical Character Recognition (OCR) enables a user to scan printed material into a computer or handheld unit. The software converts the image to text, so a text-reading program can read the written material to the user. Different programs use different scan and OCR engines. Certain programs work best with certain scanners. Also, some work better than others with replication of the image, scanning speed, form-filling capabilities, and study skills.

FREE TEXT READERS

Balabolka
by Ilya Morozov
http://www.cross-plus-a.com/balabolka.htm
- This free text-to-speech software uses Microsoft voices.
- The program can read .doc, .rtf, .pdf, and HTML files.
- Users can customize the font and background color, control the reading rate, save the sound files for future listening, and bookmark and return later.
- The software also has a spell checker and the ability to highlight homophones and correct pronunciation errors.
- It is available in 18 different languages and can be run on a USB memory stick.
- Free

Blio
by KNFB Reading Technology
http://www.blio.com
- Blio is a free software program that users can download to read eBooks with color and original layout and pictures.
- Once the book is downloaded, the reader does not have to be online.

- In addition to reading the text aloud while highlighting the words and enlarging the text, the users can insert highlights and write notes. The annotations will then be saved in the individual's virtual library.
- Readers can look up definitions and get more information on a topic online without exiting the program.
- While the software is open, users can download books that are free or shop online in the Blio bookstore for books to purchase.
- As this book is being written, Blio is only available for PCs. However, new releases are scheduled so that it can be used on additional types of computers and devices and offer more features such as different voices and adjustable speeds.
- Free

CLiCk, Speak
by Charles L. Chen
http://clickspeak.clcworld.net
- This is a free Firefox extension that reads the Internet and highlights phrases and sentences as it reads.
- Multilingual support
- Windows, Macintosh, and Linux
- Works with SAPI 5 voices such as Cepstral and NeoSpeech, which can be purchased at http://nextup.com.
- Free

Free Text-to-Speech on a Mac
- On the Mac, go to System Preferences > Speech > Text to Speech > Speak selected text when the key is pressed > Command + R.
- Whenever text is highlighted in any application and Command + R is pressed, the text will be read.
- Alex is a high-quality free Mac voice.

Narrator
by Microsoft Corporation
http://www.microsoft.com
- Windows comes with a basic screen reader called Narrator, which reads aloud text on the screen and describes some events (such as error messages appearing) that happen while you're using the computer.
- It is located in the Ease of Access Center.
- To open Narrator, click the Start button, type "Narrator" in the search box, then select Narrator from the list of results.

- It is not intended to be a fully functioning screen reader.
- Free with Windows

ReadPlease 2003
by ReadPlease
http://www.readplease.com

- This works with Microsoft voices, reads text via Windows clipboard from any program, has an adjustable voice speed (rate), and users can customize font and background color.
- The interface is easy to use, with VCR-like controls.
- Free (additional versions are available at varying costs)

VoiceOver
by Apple
http://www.apple.com/accessibility/voiceover

- VoiceOver is a screen reader that is included on the Mac OS X computer.
- Press Command+F5 to get started.
- This accessibility interface offers magnification options, keyboard control, and spoken English descriptions of what's happening on screen.
- VoiceOver reads aloud the contents of files, including web pages, mail messages, and word processing files, and provides a comprehensive audible description of the workspace, such as keyboard commands for interacting with applications and system controls.
- It can be controlled using gestures that are shared by VoiceOver on the iPhone.
- Mac OS X comes with a variety of applications that work with VoiceOver, including word processing, e-mail, web browsing, calendaring, Internet messaging software, and iTunes software. VoiceOver works with Preview, which lets you read PDFs; QuickTime, which plays movies and other media; Terminal, a UNIX command-line application; various utilities; and System Preferences.
- Available in 18 languages.
- The pronunciation dictionary can be used to replace words, change the way VoiceOver pronounces words, and manage abbreviations and special characters, such as smiley faces and other emoticons.
- In Mac OS X, you can zoom the entire screen up to 20x magnification. VoiceOver, meanwhile, allows you to independently magnify the element or contents in its cursor as large as the screen, making it easier for sighted and partially sighted users to see the text as you move the VoiceOver cursor.

- Use Tiling Visuals to remove onscreen clutter and other visual distractions. Tiling Visuals dims everything onscreen except the item or element in the VoiceOver cursor, centers that element (making it easy to find), and presents it at full brightness. You also have the option of scaling it up, so it's even easier to see.
- Free (only included on Mac OS X computers)

WordTalk
by CALL Scotland
http://www.wordtalk.org.uk/Home
- This program works within Microsoft Word and Outlook.
- It sits in the toolbar.
- Colors, voice, and speed can be customized.
- It highlights each word that is read and has a talking spell checker and thesaurus. It can save settings and users can convert their text files to a .wav or MP3 file.
- Free

TEXT READERS WITH A FEW MORE FEATURES

2nd Speech Center v3.2
by 2nd Speech Center
http://www.2ndspeechcenter.com
- This software enables the user to listen to documents, e-mails, or web pages.
- It allows for the conversion of text to MP3 or .wav files for listening on an MP3 player.
- It supports dozens of voices for multiple languages.
- Highlight the text you want read and then select Control+C and the program will read it back to you.
- Words can be highlighted as they are read aloud.
- Pronunciations can be corrected.
- Windows
- $39.95

Premier Internet Toolbar
by Premier Literacy
http://www.readingmadeeasy.com
- This multifunctional toolbar displays each time the Internet browser is opened, providing a convenient set of useful tools for accessing and capturing Internet-based information more efficiently.

- It includes a number of programs to make the Internet easy to access.
- $89.95

TextAloud3
by NextUp
http://www.nextup.com

- This software reads text aloud from e-mail, web pages, and written documents in natural sounding voices.
- Word and sentence highlighting are available so that users focus on the words as they are read aloud. The words not highlighted can be masked (dimmed) for increased focus.
- An online dictionary and English pronunciation editor for words are integrated into this software to provide assistance without exiting the program.
- Users who would like to listen to the text without seeing it can save the audio file to MP3 or Windows Media files ready for playback on multiple devices.
- There are tabs in the interface so users can easily switch between articles they are reading.
- Windows
- $29.95

Ultra Hal Text-to-Speech Reader
by Zabaware
http://www.zabaware.com

- The Ultra Hal Text-to-Speech Reader application reads documents aloud in one of its many high-quality voices.
- This program can be used for proofreading, reading eBooks, reading standard pop-up messages, and voicing clipboard contents. With this function, users can easily have it read their e-mail and the contents of websites.
- This program is also able to speak incoming instant messages aloud and convert text files into WAV audio files.
- Windows
- Free or $29.95 for a version with different voices

Universal Reader Plus
by Premier Literacy
http:// www.readingmadeeasy.com

- Universal Reader software reads aloud selected text to the user.

- It can be used to read e-mail, Word documents, and web pages.
- The user clicks on the mouth icon to read, the stoplight to stop, the yellow light to pause, and the rewind button to start over from the beginning.
- The program highlights the word as it is read.
- To make viewing easier, the text can be changed and enlarged, and colors can be altered.
- With the talking pointer, the user can place the cursor over any online text, icon, or picture and the text or a description of the image will be read aloud.
- There is a choice of voices and speeds.
- This program can translate text into several languages. A summarization feature allows users to quickly summarize the information in a document, whether it's a range of pages or an entire document.
- A Flash reader is available that can enable the user to select text that is actually an image and convert it to accessible text.
- Windows
- $79.95

VisioVoice
by AssistiveWare
http://www.assistiveware.com

- VisioVoice is helpful for blind and low vision users. An image enlarger zooms in the area around the cursor.
- It highlights words and sentences as they are spoken aloud in Microsoft Word, HTML, PDF, and RTF documents.
- VisioVoice also provides help with written expression. It can be configured to say letters and words aloud as they are typed.
- There is multilingual support.
- Users can listen to audio files on MP3 players.
- Mac
- $249.00

ADVANCED TEXT READERS WITH READING, WRITING, AND STUDYING TOOLS

E-Text Reader
by Premier Literacy
http://www.readingmadeeasy.com

- This reader offers the ability to change voices, to read at any speed, and to make notes on documents.
- The reader can highlight with four different colors.
- Users are able to extract all text highlighted in a color and save to separate files for review.
- The format of the extracted information is retained during the extraction, including graphics that are part of the highlighted text.
- Readers can save bookmarks within the documents to more easily find points of interest. Text can be made bold or underlined.
- Windows
- $79.95

Key to Access
by Premier Literacy
http://www.readingmadeeasy.com
- This enables an individual's assistive reading tools and personalized settings to be used on any Windows computer without loading the software onto the computer.
- By inserting the MP3 player into any USB port, a floating toolbar will appear, and the user can select any of the eight different tools available.
- The built-in voice recorder allows the user to dictate notes or record lectures and listen to them later.
- Windows
- $349.95

Kurzweil 3000
by Kurzweil Educational Systems
http://www.kurzweiledu.com
- Kurzweil 3000 is comprehensive reading, writing, and learning software for struggling readers.
- This program reads aloud electronic or scanned text and provides support for writing and learning with active learning, studying, and test-taking strategies.
- Delivery models for the program include standalone, network, web license, and USB.
- There is a multilanguage recognition option.
- Reading supports include:
  - o a text reader that displays words and sentences in contrasting colors;

- o the ability to read web content aloud and translate text via Google Translate;
- o a picture dictionary (with more than 1,300 graphics) for associating images with words in English and Spanish and bilingual pronunciation of words;
- o access to http://Bookshare.org, a free, searchable, online book and periodical library for students; and
- o expanded PDF functionality.

- Windows and Mac
- $1,495

Microsoft Word 2007

by Microsoft Corporation
http://www.microsoft.com

- Microsoft Word is the standard word processing software program in both the educational world and the business world.
- Word includes many learning and accessibility features of which most users are unaware.
- More information on Word's accessibility options can be found at http://www.microsoft.com/Office/system/accessibility.
- There are features included in Word that will help the reader with the following tasks: generating summaries, highlighting text, checking the readability of selected text, linking highlighted words to dictionary definitions and a thesaurus, auto summarizing of text, adjusting characters and line spacing, decluttering the toolbar and showing only the items that are frequently used, reading text-to-speech, inserting audio or text comments into documents, inserting graphics, changing the visual presentation of the text, and zooming into a portion of the page.
- The Windows Magnifier is very helpful for people with low vision. Full-screen mode magnifies the entire desktop, and lens mode zooms in on particular areas.
- A Spanish version is available.
- Windows and Mac
- $149.99 (Home and Student bundle)

Microsoft Word 2010

by Microsoft Corporation
http://www.microsoft.com

- The 2010 version offers the features of Word 2007 except for the ability to summarize written material.

- Microsoft Office Accessibility tutorials can be viewed at http://www.microsoft.com/enable/training/office2010/default.aspx.
- Actions previously found on the File menu or in the Microsoft Office button can now be found in the Microsoft Office Backstage view. By displaying more space and providing more detail about available commands, accessibility-conscious users will have more context and information about how to use commands.
- An Accessibility Checker is available to help users create more accessible content.
- Windows and Mac
- $149.99 (Home and Student bundle)

Microsoft Office Web Apps
by Microsoft Corporation
http://www.microsoft.com

- Office Web Apps include online versions of Word, Excel, PowerPoint, and OneNote. The web apps allow sharing and collaboration of documents and files and also feature user interfaces similar to their desktop counterparts.
- For Word documents it offers the ability to open the document as a tagged PDF. This allows people to use a PDF viewer that is compatible with their screen reader to read the Word document.
- Windows and Mac
- Free

Premier Literacy Productivity Pack
by Premier Literacy
http://www.readingmadeeasy.com

- The Literacy Productivity Pack bundles 10 tools plus the Premier Internet Toolbar to assist with literacy including: Scan and Read Pro, Talking Word Processor, Premier Predictor Pro, PDF Equalizer, PDF Magic Pro, Text-to-Audio, E-Text Reader, Universal Reader Plus, Ultimate Talking Dictionary, and Talking Calculator.
- The programs are available on a floating task-oriented toolbar that works with many standard applications such as Microsoft Word.
- The pack includes all of the features of the Talking Word Processor.
- Windows and Mac
- $249.95

Read&Write GOLD

by Texthelp Systems

http://www.texthelp.com

- Read&Write Gold is an easy-to-use toolbar that sits discreetly on top of any open application. It offers a wide variety of tools to help with reading, writing, and studying.
- Features to help with reading include:
  - o **Screen Masking**: Blocks any text that is not being read to provide help with concentration. Other options include: whole screen tinting and underlining the line being typed to help with tracking.
  - o **Text-to-Speech**: Simple and accurate way to read text from word documents, e-mail, and the web. Audio-visual reinforcement provided when the option for words to be highlighted is chosen. High-quality, natural sounding voices are available.
  - o **PDF Aloud**: Enables user to read PDF files.
  - o **Scanning**: OCR facilities are provided that allow the user to scan a text document such as letter or a page from a book and convert it into a readable format.
  - o **Screenshot Reader**: Makes on-screen text accessible with the option to save it to Word.

- Additional helpful features include: phonetic spell checker and homophone checker that picks up more complicated errors than standard spell checkers; word prediction; dictionary with definitions; web highlighting; Daisy Reader (format for people who are blind or print disabled); Word Wizard (acts as a thesaurus, providing a choice of alternative words); a study skills toolbar; calculator; Speechmaker (text conversion into audio file); PDF Aloud (makes PDFs accessible for text-to-speech); and research tools like a fact finder, fact folder, and fact mapper.
- Windows and Mac
- $645.00

Read:OutLoud

by Don Johnston

http://www.donjohnston.com

- Read:OutLoud is a text reader created with students in mind that supports individuals with modeling, scaffolding, and practice of reading strategies to comprehend text.

- Includes an accessible web browser that is compatible on Mac and Windows. It highlights word-by-word as it reads.
- Compatible with all common accessible book formats. Opens NIMAS and DAISY 3 files without converting the files to preserve key navigation and description information from the NIMAS file.
- Users can capture critical facts and information with green, red, and yellow highlighters. Highlighted text is automatically added to an outline that can be organized, modified, and used for studying or report writing.
- The bibliographer helps students create their own bibliography using dozens of source types including electronic/webpage, articles, and books, in both MLA and APA format.
- Features the latest Acapela voices.
- This software can also be purchased in a bundle with other software that assists with writing, such as Don Johnston's Draft:Builder and Co:Writer.
- Windows and Mac
- $319.00

WordQ
by Quillsoft
http://www.wordq.com

- WordQ is a software tool used along with standard writing software. There is no need to cut and paste onto a clipboard.
- It can read aloud letters, words, and sentences—or an entire document—and offers word prediction.
- WordQ is intentionally designed to be as simple as possible and any nonpriority features are not included by design.
- If the user can manually highlight text in a browser, then WordQ will read aloud the online text after pressing the Read button or pressing F11.
- A variety of voices is available, and the speed at which the text is read can be controlled.
- This software can be used with SpeakQ, which is a simplified word recognition software.
- Windows and Mac
- $199.00

WYNN Literacy Software
by Freedom Scientific
http://www.freedomscientific.com

- WYNN uses four color-coded rotating toolbars.

- There are many supports for the reading process, including:
  - o bimodal approach to reading (text is highlighted in context as it is spoken aloud in a natural sounding voice);
  - o scanned-in pages retain original layout;
  - o customized visual presentation;
  - o built-in talking dictionary and thesaurus;
  - o traditional study tools like highlighting, bookmarking, and text and voice notes;
  - o ability to read the Internet, highlight web pages, and extract highlighted text;
  - o a built-in pop-up blocker to allow the student to focus;
  - o an enhanced Webmasking feature for customization while reading web pages;
  - o ability to read hyperlinks without activating them;
  - o RealSpeak Solo provides high-quality, human-sounding voices;
  - o digital talking books (DAISY and NIMAS books) support is included;
  - o one-click PDF file conversion;
  - o preferred auditory reading environments (e.g., pause between sentences, numerous voices, speed of reading, immediate stop and start, and multiple languages);
  - o MP3 and WAV conversion; and
  - o compatibility with WebCT (an online proprietary virtual learning environment system).

- There are two products:
  - o **WYNN Wizard** is a scanning and reading software that includes OCR to scan printed pages and convert them into electronic text. Speech synthesis enables this scanned text to be read aloud. Additionally, WYNN Wizard can read word processing documents, Adobe Acrobat PDF files, text files, and the Internet. $995.00
  - o **WYNN Reader** includes all features of WYNN Wizard except OCR. Files that have been previously scanned and saved using WYNN Wizard can be read with WYNN Reader. $375.00

PICTURE-BASED, TALKING WORD PROCESSORS

People with severe reading deficits who are unable to use text-based word processors to read are often able to benefit from picture-based, talking word processors. These programs typically offer speech feedback, symbols, or pictures to support text and on-screen grids. These programs enable the therapist, teacher, or parent to create reading activities specifically suited to individuals, incorporating as many or as few pictures and sound support as needed.

Clicker 5
by Crick Software
http://www.cricksoft.com/us/products/clicker

- Clicker is a powerful and easy-to-use multimedia tool.
- Listening to the text while studying the picture helps to introduce new words and develop understanding.
- Many premade talking books are available to support literacy.
- Planet Wobble is a reading series for struggling readers that contains 21 graded Clicker talking books and includes printed copies of the books, plus Clicker writing activities.
- Find Out and Write About is a nonfiction series that covers many curriculum areas and has linked writing activities from every page.
- Users can hear words in the Clicker Grid before writing or proofread after writing. The words are highlighted as they are spoken.
- Animation, digital recordings, a variety of software voices, and video can be used.
- Clicker comes with an extensive picture library of 1,800 items.
- Full switch access is provided.
- In addition to the high-quality speech, the clean, uncluttered screen layout, and the customizable color-coded grids, Clicker includes a range of extensive accessibility options for users with low vision.
- A very helpful support network includes access to http://www.learninggrids.com, which features many of grid sets that can be accessed directly from the program. Many curriculum-based activities are available for download.
- Windows and Mac
- $249.00

Communicate: SymWriter
by DynaVox Mayer-Johnson
http://www.mayerjohnson.com

- Communicate: SymWriter is a talking word processor that uses symbols to help learners of all ages and abilities read and write.
- Features more than 9,000 Picture Communication Symbols (PCS) and more than 8,000 Widgit Literacy Symbols (WLS).

- Increases comprehension with images that correspond with words.
- Windows
- $229.00

PictureIt
by Slater Software
http://www.slatersoftware.com

- The software features automatic picture-word matching for creating picture assisted reading.
- Users can turn any document into an eBook using Reader Mode.
- It includes more than 10,500 Literacy Support Pictures, plus the user can import photos and clip art.
- Users can choose voices, rates, and pronunciations for the assisted reading program.
- The program is available in Spanish.
- Windows and Mac
- $295.00

ALTERNATIVE BOOK FORMATS

There are several ways to read a book other than the traditional paper format. Audiobooks are narrated by a human voice. Braille books are provided for people who are blind. Interactive talking books can be used to improve reading skills.

An increasing number of books are now available in electronic format. The book's content may be available on a CD, by scanning with OCR, or by download. DAISY is the international digital talking book standard, which provides the capability to distribute books digitally. NIMAS is a national standard by which publishers are required to provide textbook files.

One benefit of a digital format for individuals with language and learning challenges is the ability to change the appearance of the text. The way the reader sees the text can have a profound impact on comprehension. Cluttered pages with little white space and small print make reading more difficult. With eBooks, it's often helpful to enlarge the font and increase the color contrast of the text and background to make on-screen reading easier. When text is provided electronically, it can be imported into text readers and talking word processors.

Accessible Book Collection

http://www.accessiblebookcollection.org

- This is a subscription-based service with a high-interest, low reading level. It offers detailed information on the reading level for each title.
- The primary audience is youth with learning disabilities.
- Intellipics and Clicker formatted picture books are available.
- Tools are available so that the text size, color, and spacing of eBooks can be changed.
- Individuals are eligible if they have a documented disability that prevents them from reading standard print effectively.
- Windows and Mac
- The cost of an annual subscription is $49.95.

BookBox

http://www.bookbox.com

- This resource is most appropriate for children.
- BookBox includes downloadable Flash stories that are digitally narrated with simple animation and streaming text across the bottom.
- It synchronizes text, audio, and visual media to create an educational and entertaining reading experience.
- The reader sees whole phrases, and the letters go from white to red as the words are spoken.
- The stories are available in multiple languages.
- Many stories are available for download for $2.99 each, while CDs with several stories are approximately $12.99.

Bookshare

http://www.bookshare.org

- Bookshare is free for all U.S. students with a documented print disability. It is available by paid subscription for others with undocumented print disabilities who wish to join.
- It offers a searchable online library of approximately 90,000 digital books, textbooks, and periodicals.
- The digital downloads can be read using free software for DAISY digital books. Membership includes free version of Humanware's Victor Reader Soft Bookshare Edition and Don Johnston's READ:OutLoud Bookshare Edition.
- Hard copy braille books can be created with an embosser.
- Free

Digital Book Index
http://www.digitalbookindex.org
- Digital Book Index provides links to more than 165,000 full-text digital books from more than 1,800 commercial and noncommercial publishers, universities, and various private sites.
- More than 140,000 of these books, texts, and documents are available for free, while many others are available at a very modest cost.

Disney Digital Books
https://disneydigitalbooks.go.com
- Users can access more than 600 books.
- Digital pages can be turned with a Magic Pen.
- Children can hear stories read aloud with Look and Listen Books.
- Users can create original stories with the Story-Builder option.
- $1.99 per book (or you can purchase a subscription by creating an account)

International Children's Digital Library (ICDL)
http://www.childrenslibrary.org
- THE ICDL Foundation's goal is to create a collection of books that represents outstanding historical and contemporary books from throughout the world. Ultimately, the Foundation aspires to have every culture and language represented so that every child can know and appreciate the riches of children's literature from the world community.
- The ICDL collection includes more than 4,000 books in 54 languages.
- There are also books available for iPad/iPhone.
- Free

National Library Service for the Blind and Physically Handicapped (NLS)
http://www.loc.gov/nls
- This is a free service of the Library of Congress that is commonly referred to as Talking Books.
- NLS offers leisure materials and magazines on an audiocassette or audio disk. The collection includes popular novels, classical literature, poetry, biographies, and magazines.
- Talking Books are distributed through a network of regional and subregional libraries.
- Free

Pacecar
http://pacecar.missingmethod.com
- Pacecar is an online reading tool designed to help individuals read faster and with more focus by masking the distracting elements on the page, creating a reading window.
- Users drag the Pacecar bookmarklet into their browser's bookmarks toolbar. When users want to read a page with Pacecar, they just click on it.
- At the time of this book's writing, it was only compatible with the Firefox browser.
- Free

Project Gutenberg
http://www.gutenberg.org
- More than 33,000 free eBooks are available to read on the PC, iPad, Kindle, Sony Reader, iPhone, Android, or other portable devices.
- No fee or registration is required.
- All books are free in the United States because their copyright has expired.
- An online book catalogue is available and users can browse by author, title, language, or recently posted.
- Books are available in many languages.
- Free

RAZ-Kids Online Leveled Reading Library
http://www.raz-kids.com
- Users can benefit from listening for modeled fluency, reading for practice, recording their reading, and checking comprehension with the quizzes.
- Learning A-Z licenses are sold on a per classroom basis, which is what a parent should select if ordering for home use. Each registered teacher can use the license with up to 36 students in one classroom.
- Contact the company for pricing information.

Recording for the Blind and Dyslexic (RFB&D)
http://www.rfbd.org
- This is a nonprofit service organization that provides free access to the nation's largest audiobook library of human narrated educational books (academic textbooks) and nonfiction books on audiocassette and CD.

- Various audiobook downloadable formats, including DAISY and WMA (Windows Media Audio) are available. The books can be synced to MP3 players with Digital Rights Management (DRM) capabilities to play encrypted content.
- The ReadHear software player for Mac and Windows enables users to listen to audio books on the computer.
- RFB&D Individual Membership is free to individuals with a print disability. A print disability can be a learning disability, a visual impairment, or a physical disability. Certification is required; certification options are located within the online registration process.

Simple English Wikipedia
http://simple.wikipedia.org
- Wikipedia's Simple English entries scaffold the reader by using straightforward language, by chunking the information, and by providing links for further inquiry.
- Simple English is listed under the language options.
- Free

Storyline Online
http://www.storylineonline.net
- The site features video streaming of stories read aloud by actors, allowing readers to follow along with the text.
- The site includes suggestions for related activities.
- Free

Tar Heel Reader
http://www.tarheelreader.org
- This site includes a collection of easy-to-read books on a wide variety of topics.
- Each book is switch-accessible and speech enabled.
- They may be downloaded as a slideshow in PowerPoint, Impress, or Flash format.
- It is appropriate for beginning readers of all ages, including adolescents.
- Free

TumbleBookLibrary
http://tumblebooks.com
- This is an online collection of animated, talking picture books for young children.

- The site also offers read-along books for adolescents and adults.
- It offers a variety of Apple apps.
- $399 per year for library or school subscriptions

ADAPTED ONLINE NEWSPAPERS

News-2-You
http://www.news-2-you.com
- This is a weekly Internet-based picture newspaper that features current events and other articles of interest.
- There are four editions: simplified, regular, higher, and advanced.
- Two communication boards can also be downloaded each week with pertinent vocabulary.
- Articles about world news are displayed on an interactive Google map.
- Many downloadable activity pages are included as well as web-based games.
- $140.00 for a single subscription for one year

NewsCurrents
http://www.newscurrents.com
- NewsCurrents is a current events newspaper with accompanying discussion guides for classroom use.
- It's written on three levels of difficulty and is available online or on DVD.
- $199 for an online subscription that includes a weekly issue (for 34 weeks of the year) with images corresponding to five or six stories in that week's news.

NewsLink
http://www.newslink.org
- This is the Internet's most comprehensive news resource, with nearly 20,000 free media links.
- Free

Onlinenewspapers.com
http://www.onlinenewspapers.com
- This site links to thousands of world newspapers for free.
- Free

PORTABLE EBOOK READERS

The use of portable eBook readers has gained momentum in mainstream society. eBooks can be wonderful assistive technology tools that, when paired with effective instruction and guidance, can greatly help individuals who have reading challenges. eBook readers are gaining in popularity due to these improving features:

- ✓ People can store many books, magazines, and newspapers in a very small, lightweight device that is easy to carry.
- ✓ Some devices (such as the Kindle) can read aloud the books using text-to-speech or recorded voices.
- ✓ New e-ink technology makes reading very easy on the eyes.
- ✓ Prices have dropped.
- ✓ The readers now have a longer battery life.
- ✓ The devices have improved ease of use.
- ✓ Many offer the ability to purchase books directly from the device rather than as a transfer from a computer.
- ✓ Some devices are compatible with book formats for library books and books from sources such as http://www.bookshare.org.
- ✓ Apps are now available for PCs and Macs, tablets such as the iPad, and cell phones so that books can be read from more than one device.
- ✓ Users can typically change the font size.
- ✓ Many offer bookmarking and annotation features.
- ✓ Some devices (such as the Nook) allow readers to share books.

This world of more affordable, fully featured eBook readers is changing fast and will continue to improve. There can now also be a social component to reading. More and more hybrids are being developed that function as eBook readers but also allow the user to access the Internet and offer word processing capabilities. On some of the devices, such as the Kindle, it is possible for users to use social networking sites such as Twitter and Facebook to post their notes and the text as they highlight while reading.

Below is a list of popular eBook readers. An online search will reveal many more. One important feature to look for to help individuals with reading challenges is their ability to read the books while the eBook reader uses text-to-speech, such as with the Kindle 3. Please be sure to keep in mind that in some cases the publishers of the books will not permit this to happen. The books being read aloud with text-to-speech sound very different from audiobooks that have people reading the books aloud rather than a computer—which in many cases can sound very much like a human.

It's also helpful to be able to access the widest variety of books. The ePub format is needed to read library books. Some readers are able to be used in direct sunlight such as the Kindle 3 and newest versions of the Nook, while others use background lighting and have a glare in direct light. Additional features that some of these devices offer are color and the ability to watch videos and listen to music.

- ✓ **Alex eReaders**: http://www.springdesign.com
- ✓ **BeBook Neo**: http://mybebook.com
- ✓ **ECTACO jetBook LITE**: http://www.jetbook.net
- ✓ **iPad**: http://www.apple.com
- ✓ **Kindle**: http://www.amazon.com
- ✓ **Nook**: http://www.barnesandnoble.com
- ✓ **Sony Digital Book Reader**: http://www.sonystyle.com

READING ALOUD HANDHELD DEVICES

There are an increasing number of affordable portable devices in addition to some of the eBook readers mentioned earlier that can read aloud to help individuals who are unable to read.

AnyBook Reader
by Franklin Electronic Publishers
http://www.franklin.com

- The AnyBook Reader is a device that looks like a pen, but functions more like a digital recorder when used with a special collection of stickers.
- While in the record mode, the person recording touches a sticker with the pen and then records a message. Each sticker has a unique code that is then linked with the audio file. When the listener is in play mode, he touches the sticker and listens to the recording play back.
- No text is involved except that the device is supposed to be placed on pages on a book so that a child can hear a parent reading the book aloud to them.
- The stickers can be used creatively to help users sequence steps in a task, listen to instructions, or provide reminders.
- 2 AAA batteries are required and not included when the pen is purchased.
- The 15-hour edition costs $39.99; the 60-hour edition is $59.99

ClassMate Reader

by HumanWare

http://www.humanware.com

- The ClassMate Reader is designed to improve reading skills.
- It includes an SD card with sample content reading material.
- It reads aloud and simultaneously displays and highlights text on its full color screen.
- Users can use text or voice notes within the text to help with comprehension. The notes can then be extracted and sent to a computer.
- It is customizable.
- $519.00

Intel Reader

http://www.reader.intel.com

- The Intel Reader is a mobile handheld device that combines a high-resolution camera with an Intel Atom processor. It converts printed text to digital text, and then reads it aloud while highlighting the text onscreen.
- Users point, shoot, and listen to quickly access printed text such as schoolwork, work material, or menus on the spot.
- It does not require sight to operate.
- For people with low vision, the large screen display can zoom in and out and text size can easily be adjusted.
- It weighs just over a pound and is about the size of a paperback book.
- The Intel Reader will play most content, including MP3s, DAISY books, and text files transferred from a computer, and it has built-in features to help manage content.
- The Intel Reader can generate audio versions of printed materials, such as MP3s, that can be played on most digital music players or computers.
- DAISY digital talking books and other audiobooks can be loaded from computers and other devices, so users can keep and manage their content in one place.
- $1,495

kReader Mobile

by KNFB Reading Technology

http://www.knfbreader.com

- This software places the functionality of a reading machine into a multifunction cell phone.

- The user takes a photo of the print material to be read and the character recognition software in conjunction with high-quality text-to-speech will read the contents of the document aloud. At the same time, it can display the print on the phone's built-in screen and highlight each word as it is spoken.
- Requires that the phone carrier supports unlocked GSM phones (in the U.S. that includes AT&T and T-Mobile).
- Pricing is available from vendors listed on the website.

PEARL
by Freedom Scientific
http://www.freedomscientific.com

- This is a portable reading device that converts printed text to human-like speech in seconds.
- The PEARL camera connects to a PC, and users press a keystroke to snap a picture and hear their documents read back to them with synthesized speech while they control the reading rate and voice.
- There is an automatic mode that senses motion and snaps an image whenever a page is turned.
- The PEARL can be used to read books, newspapers, magazines, and bills. OpenBook identifies columns and places them in logical reading order.
- Reads aloud in multiple languages.
- Multiple options are available for low vision users.
- Individual words can be spotlighted as they are spoken.
- $1,195.00

Reading Pens
by Wizcom Technologies
http://www.wizcomtech.com

- There are several portable scanners and pens that use text-to-speech software to offer word-by-word pronunciation of scanned words, lines of text, definitions, and synonyms through an integrated speaker or headphones.
- They generally require good manual dexterity, vision, and cognitive skills for functional use.
- Pens differ in their scanning speeds. Prices vary depending on selected features.
- $229.95–$279.95

RNIB PenFriend Voice Labeling System
http://www.independentliving.com

- Allows users to easily record and rerecord information onto self-adhesive labels.
- This small pen-shaped recorder provides easy recognition sound and just four buttons in a simple identifiable pattern.
- Users can instantly play back the recordings; no computer is required.
- This device can be made to record instructions or leave voice messages. It can also be used as a portable note taker.
- There is no limit to the record length associated with each label.
- More than 70 hours of recording time is available on 1 GB of internal memory.
- $139.95

CHAPTER 8

TECHNOLOGY TO IMPROVE READING SKILLS

LANGUAGE-BASED READING SKILLS

There are many computer software programs and mobile apps that use a drill-and-practice approach to improve reading skills. Most of these programs:

- ✓ offer tasks at a variety of reading levels,
- ✓ can be customized,
- ✓ provide immediate feedback regarding the accuracy of the response, and
- ✓ document performance.

Keep in mind that new versions of software are frequently being released and features are often changed. It is important to review websites for more up-to-date and in-depth analysis of product comparisons. Available products are listed here in three categories:

- ✓ software to load onto a computer or that plays from a CD/DVD,
- ✓ online programs, and
- ✓ apps that can be used on handhelds such as a phone, iPod touch, or iPad.

SOFTWARE TO LOAD ONTO A COMPUTER OR THAT PLAYS FROM A CD/DVD

Aphasia Tutor 1: Words +Out Loud and Aphasia Tutor 2: Sentences +Out Loud
by Bungalow Software
http://www.bungalowsoftware.com

- The exercises in these programs progress in difficulty from words to phrases and then to sentence-level reading comprehension tasks.
- The text is large and the program is easy to use for people with severe deficits.
- The software is most appropriate for adults, but some children find it less distracting than software that is developed for children with graphics, color, and sounds.
- Windows
- $149.50 for home program; $50.00 as part of a monthly subscription

Aphasia Tutor 3: Story Reading
by Bungalow Software
http://www.bungalowsoftware.com

- This program improves reading comprehension at the paragraph and story levels.
- Lessons gradually increase in passage length and question complexity (including factual and inferential questions).
- The software is most appropriate for adults, but some children may find it less distracting than other programs.
- Windows
- $99.50 for home program; $50.00 as part of a monthly subscription

Aphasia Tutor 4: Functional Reading
by Bungalow Software
http://www.bungalowsoftware.com

- This software provides realistic reading materials such as medicine labels, want ads, and television guides.
- The software is most appropriate for adults.
- Windows
- $69.50 for the home program; $50.00 as part of a monthly subscription

Bailey's Book House for Home
by Edmark
http://www.k12software.com

- This program was designed for children who are in preschool through second grade.
- Children build a reading and writing foundation by exploring letters, words, rhyming, and sentence building.
- Users practice skills in word recognition, phonics, comprehension, phonemic awareness, written expression, vocabulary development, and word building.
- Windows and Mac
- $15.95

Boost
by Sound Reading Solutions
http://www.soundreading.com

- The software has more than 25 activities that cover all aspects of learning to read well from memory and attention to word identification.
- Windows and Mac
- $189.00

BrainPro and BrainSpark
by Scientific Learning
http://www.brainsparklearning.com

- These programs are designed for students and use exercises from the Fast ForWord family of products to improve sequencing, processing rate, attention, recall and memory, and knowledge.
- BrainPro was developed for struggling students and uses tutors to monitor the users' progress and provide guidance to parents or teachers.
- BrainSpark was developed for children who are reading at or above grade level.
- Windows and Mac
- Contact providers on the website for pricing.

ClozePro Version 2
by Crick Software
http://www.cricksoft.com/us/products/clozepro

- The teacher, therapist, or parent selects a body of text that can be either typed or copied from a website, e-mail, or document. He or she then chooses words to remove from the text to create a wide variety of activities.

- The missing words can be given in a grid at the bottom of the page or in a multiple-choice format.
- The user then selects words to place back into the text.
- This program offers customizable interfaces, support features, differentiation options, and detailed reporting capability to track progress, and it is fully switch-accessible.
- Many free downloadable activities that can be used with this software are available at http://www.learninggrids.com.
- Windows and Mac
- $199.00 for a single computer

Earobics
by Cognitive Concepts
http://www.donjohnston.com and http://www.enablemart.com

- There are two versions, each of which offers hundreds of levels of instruction.
- Each level is specially developed to help students build critical literacy skills, including recognizing and blending sounds, rhyming, and discriminating phonemes within words.
- Windows and Mac
- $65.00 (home version)

Edmark Reading Program–Software Version
by Edmark
http://www.donjohnston.com and http://www.proedinc.com

- Using a whole word approach, this program teaches recognition and comprehension of words with built-in instructions, audio cues, and feedback.
- The Level 1 software version teaches 150 words chosen from the Dolch Word List for first-grade readers, as well as "-s," "-ed," and "-ing" endings; capitalization; and punctuation.
- Level 2 teaches 200 words, including compound words, and reviews and reinforces words learned in Level 1. At 10-word intervals, a review and test activities are provided.
- Windows and Mac
- $429.00 per level

Fast ForWord
by Scientific Learning
http://www.scilearn.com

- This is a reading intervention program for schools and clinical specialists who help students who are struggling and reading below grade level.
- It offers programs that feature a sequenced learning environment that advances cognitive skills in the context of appropriate reading skills.
- Windows and Mac
- Provided by trained providers. Contact company for pricing.

HearBuilder Phonological Awareness
by Super Duper Publications
http://www.hearbuilder.com

- This gives students a systematic way to improve auditory and phonological awareness skills. Students use the phonics activities to earn band members and instruments for their rock band.
- Users complete increasingly difficult sound awareness tasks and work to demonstrate understanding in nine areas: sentence segmentation, syllable blending, syllable segmentation, rhyming, phoneme blending, phoneme segmentation and identification, phoneme deletion, phoneme addition, and phoneme manipulation.
- Windows and Mac
- $69.95 for home edition

Hop, Skip & Jump
by Sound Reading Solutions
http://www.soundreading.com

- This is designed for pre-K, kindergarten, and first-grade children who are emerging readers.
- The software develops preword, word, and sentence reading, as well as printed and spoken word fluency.
- Twenty activities develop phonemic awareness, sound discrimination, auditory attention, and memory for comprehension.
- Windows and Mac
- $249.00

Lexia Reading Software

by Lexia Learning Systems

http://www.lexia4home.com

- Lexia offers several programs for different ages that build strength in phonemic awareness, sound-symbol correspondence, decoding, fluency, phonics, and vocabulary.
- Lexia Early Reading is for ages 4–6, Lexia Primary Reading is for ages 5–8, and Lexia Strategies for Older Students is for ages 9–adult.
- The software is based on the Orton-Gillingham method of reading remediation.
- A web-enabled version offers a school-to-home connection.
- Spanish and English directions support English language learners.
- Technical support is provided by the Family Literacy Program, not Lexia.
- Windows and Mac
- $159.95 for the first student for one year and $99.00 for each additional student in the same family for one year

Merit Software

http://www.meritsoftware.com

- This company's products cover the core reading skills through interactive exercises that use contextual help with text-to-speech technology.
- They offer a variety of products categorized by grade level as well as subject.
- Windows
- Early Reading Booster—$79.00 (home user)
- Reading Comprehension Booster— $79.00 (home user)
- Developing Critical Thinking Skills for Effective Reading— $79.00 (home user)

On Track Reading Series

by Tool Factory

http://www.toolfactory.com

- The On Track Reading Series is a five-CD set, with each disc isolating a single skill required for the development of fluent reading. Students begin with visual tracking using Eye Track, then work their way forward to formulating complete sentences using Word Track.

- Eye Track provides exercises to develop visual discrimination and spatial orientation and improve visual figure ground skills. Other activities cover visual discrimination, visual memory, and visual closure.
- Word Track shows a sentence on the screen while it is spoken aloud. It then disappears, and the user tracks each word by clicking the correct words, in order, from amongst a string of other words. The appropriate punctuation mark must also be tracked. After tracking, students type the sentence with correct capitalization and punctuation.
- Windows and Mac
- $299.95 (single user); individual tracks can also be purchased

Picture Stories and Language Activities Interactive Software
by Linguisystems
http://www.linguisystems.com
- This software was developed to help children ages 3–8 learn to anticipate, predict, and follow a storyline.
- Stories are narrated. The parent or teacher can select literacy activities such as answering yes or no questions, identifying vocabulary, and matching text to pictures.
- Windows and Mac
- $59.95

Reader Rabbit Series
by The Learning Company
http://www.broderbund.com
- This series includes a variety of affordable mainstream software for children.
- Activities involve working through puzzles, games, stories, and more with Reader Rabbit while practicing reading and language skills.
- Windows and Mac
- $9.99–$19.99

Reading Assistant
by Scientific Learning
http://www.scilearn.com
- Reading Assistant Expanded Edition software uses oral reading practice, voice recognition, intervention strategies, and quizzes to help students improve reading fluency, vocabulary, and comprehension.

- This software "listens" to a person as he or she reads aloud. It highlights words that are read aloud incorrectly and models appropriate answers as needed.
- Windows and Mac
- Reading Assistant is available for purchase from trained specialists. Contact Scientific Learning for pricing.

Reading Comprehension Level 1 Interactive Software
by Abigail Hanrahan and Catherine McSweeny
http://www.linguisystems.com
- This program uses short passages with engaging screen designs.
- There are five readability levels and 11 comprehension skills.
- Windows and Mac
- $41.95

Reading Detective Software
by The Critical Thinking Co.
http://www.criticalthinking.com
- This software develops the analysis, synthesis, and vocabulary skills needed for reading comprehension.
- There are several different versions of this software targeted for different age groups and abilities.
- The activities help users understand reading concepts such as drawing inferences, determining cause and effect, and using context clues to define vocabulary.
- Three levels are provided. At each level, users read and analyze short pieces of literature, both fiction and nonfiction. They then answer multiple-choice questions, citing evidence to support their answers.
- Windows and Mac
- $29.99 for a single-user CD

Remedy
by Sound Reading Solutions
http://www.soundreading.com
- This is designed for older students and adults.
- Remedy has more than 20 different activities from multisyllable word instruction to Read-Sound Out-Read exercises.
- Windows and Mac
- $249.00

RocketReader

by RocketReader

http://www.RocketReader.com

- Several products are available to increase reading speed, comprehension, and reading stamina.
- RocketReader improves your reading speed and comprehension with an effective combination of exercises, flash training, speed training, practice reading, and timed tests.
- The software runs only on Windows, but the online versions work on Windows, Mac, or Linux.
- $129.00 for single user download

Simon Sounds It Out (S.I.O.)

by Don Johnston

http://www.donjohnston.com

- Simon S. I. O. provides multilevel phonics practice by working on the alphabet, letters, sounds, and words. Users can pick a lesson targeting beginning sounds, ending sounds, or both.
- Users learn sounds and build, discriminate, and recall words.
- There are 31 levels of difficulty and built-in single switch scanning is available.
- Windows and Mac
- $159.00

Spotlight on Reading & Listening Comprehension
Levels 1 and 2 Software

by Linda Bowers, Rosemary Huisingh, Carolyn LoGuidice, Paul F. Johnson, and Jane Orman

http://www.linguisystems.com

- This program includes more than 60 narrated stories and 480 multiple-choice questions.
- Users listen to and read aloud with each story and its follow-up questions and answers.
- Narrated audio can be turned on and off at any time.
- Each story screen includes a full-color picture to help visual learners attach meaning to the text. Users can review the text of the story as they answer comprehension questions.
- Windows and Mac
- $59.95

Start-to-Finish Library and Core Content

by Don Johnston

http://www.donjohnston.com

- This is an accessible book collection developed for older elementary and early adolescent students reading below grade level.
- There is a wide selection of age-appropriate narrative chapter books written at two readability levels and delivered in three media formats—paperback, audio, and computer.
- Users practice reading fluently and with comprehension using multiple texts and electronic supports.
- The computer books offer a comprehension quiz after each chapter and work on reading fluency.
- Windows and Mac
- $39.99 for each computer book

Thinking Reader

by Tom Snyder Productions

http://www.tomsnyder.com

- Thinking Reader is a program that systematically builds reading comprehension skills using core, authentic literature.
- It embeds prompts, hints, model answers, and instant feedback into the text to provide individualized instruction.
- Users practice seven scientifically proven reading comprehension strategies while they read.
- Windows and Mac
- $250.00

Understanding Questions +Out Loud

by Bungalow Software

http://www.bungalowsoftware.com

- This program provides practice with understanding who, what, when, where, why, and how questions. Auditory cues can be given for support as needed.
- It displays a question and up to four answers. The user reads the question and selects an appropriate response.
- Windows
- $139.50 for home user; $50.00 as part of a monthly subscription

WordMaker

by Don Johnston

http://www.donjohnston.com

- This program provides phonics, phonemic awareness, and spelling activities to build core reading strategies.
- Students manipulate letters to make words, helping them discover words' patterns, and then sort the words into rhymes and use the rhymes to decode and spell new words. The 140 lessons included in this software give users word manipulation practice.
- Students build on the words they know how to read and spell to create new words that are longer and more difficult.
- Windows and Mac
- $159.00

ONLINE PROGRAMS

Between the Lions

by PBS Kids

http://pbskids.org/lions

- This site offers many easily accessible activities that contain vocabulary words and phonics.
- Each of the games provides visual and auditory help for users with cognitive and learning challenges.
- Free

Browser Books

by Kathy Cassidy

http://staff.prairiesouth.ca/~cassidy.kathy/browserbooks/index.htm

- This is a site for beginner readers with engaging colorful photographs.
- Online books are sorted by level and subject.
- After selecting a book, children can read them on their own or click on words to have them read aloud in natural sounding children's voices.
- Readers turn the page by clicking on a triangle.
- Free

Explode The Code

by CurriculaWorks

http://www.explodethecode.com

- This is a comprehensive curriculum for grades K–4 and an online version of a phonics program that has been available for more than 30 years, helping students build the essential literacy skills needed for reading success: phonological awareness, decoding, vocabulary, comprehension, fluency, and spelling.
- Explode The Code online activities are labeled by book, lesson, and unit.
- $55.00 yearly subscription for one student

GameGoo

by Earobics

http://www.earobics.com/gamegoo/index.html

- GameGoo features a kids' page with 13 colorful activity links divided into three levels: beginner, intermediate, and advanced.
- Most of the activities use phonic elements, such as alphabet order, letter recognition, letter-sound correspondence, and spelling.
- Free

Headsprout Early Reading

by Headsprout

http://www.headsprout.com

- The basic component skills and strategies necessary for reading, such as phonemic awareness (the sounds within words), print awareness, phonics, sounding out, segmenting, and blending, are practiced in a fun, self-directed manner.
- The second half of the program focuses more on reading vocabulary, fluency, and comprehension, while still teaching more sounds and sight words.
- The program includes 80 online episodes and ready-to-read printable stories.
- $198.00

Headsprout Reading Comprehension

by Headsprout

http://www.headsprout.com

- This program includes fifty 30-minute online lessons that teach students strategies to master the four main components of comprehension: finding facts, making inferences, identifying themes and the main idea, and learning vocabulary in context.

- $99.00

Into the Book
http://reading.ecb.org

- This is a reading comprehension resource for K–4 students and teachers.
- The site focuses on eight research-based strategies: using prior knowledge, making connections, questioning, visualizing, inferring, summarizing, evaluating, and synthesizing.
- Free

Lexercise
by Mind inFormation
http://www.lexercise.com

- Lexercise is a clinician-supervised web-based learning tool for children ages 6–16 with language-literacy disorders.
- It teaches alphabetic phonics through individualized, sequential, and multisensory exercises.
- This interactive web-based platform allows the clinician to customize and monitor research-based treatment exercises that have all of the motivational appeal of flash-based games.
- Clinician access is free with a code from the company; clients (parents) have to pay a subscription fee, which can be determined by contacting the company.

Lexia Reading
by Lexia Learning
http://www.lexialearning.com

- Lexia Reading's software helps students ages 4–adult acquire and improve essential reading skills, while supporting educators in monitoring and informing reading instruction in classrooms, schools, and districtwide. It includes an auto placement tool, helping new students to quickly begin using Lexia at their individual skill level.
- The software includes Lexia Early Reading, Lexia Primary Reading, and Lexia Strategies for Older Students.
- The programs are available to families when the school is using Lexia software.
- $159.95 for the first student for one year and $99 for each additional student in the same family for one year

Literactive

http://www.literactive.com

- Literactive offers free online reading material for preschool, kindergarten, and first-grade students.
- The program is comprised of carefully leveled animated guided readers, comprehensive phonics activities, and supplemental reading material.
- A complete phonemic and syllabic breakdown of every word in the stories is provided, enabling each child to decode the written text working alone or in small classroom groups.
- ESL versions of the reading material are available for download.
- Starting with initial nursery rhymes, the site moves students through prereading activities, alphabet awareness, letter sounds, short vowels, consonant-vowel-consonant word blending, initial blends, long vowels, and all of the phonics activities critical for developing early reading skills.
- Free

Parrot Software

by Parrot Software

http://www.parrotsoftware.com

- Parrot offers approximately 70 programs with its online subscription for Windows and Mac users. Many of them work to improve reading as well as cognition and communication.
- A trial version is available at http://www.parrotsoftware.com/Trial/misc/programselector.aspx, which won't expire. It is intended for professionals who want to figure out which programs are most appropriate for users. It does not track performance or personalize feedback like the programs for subscribers.
- Some of the Parrot programs that work on reading skills are: Antonym and Synonyms, Picture Identification, Reading Comprehension, Picture Association, Sentence Completion, Sorting by Category, Traffic Signs, Verbal Analogies, and Word Association.
- $24.95 per month

RAZ-Kids Online Leveled Reading Library

by Learning A–Z

http://www.raz-kids.com

- Users benefit from listening for modeled fluency, reading for practice, recording their reading, and checking comprehension with quizzes.

- Learning A-Z licenses are sold on a per classroom basis, which is what a parent should select if ordering for home use. Each teacher paid and registered can use the license with up to 36 students in one classroom.
- $79.95 for a year-long subscription

Scholastic
http://www2.scholastic.com
- Select "Student Activities" then "Computer Lab Favorites."
- Users can then browse the online activities by grade and subject.
- There is a wide range of wonderful activities for children on this site.
- Free

Time4Learning
by Time4Learning
http://www.time4learning.com
- This site provides home-based online learning from pre-K to eighth grade.
- The reading programs teach and improve phonemic awareness, phonics, reading fluency, vocabulary, and comprehension.
- The language arts program teaches reading comprehension, fluency, vocabulary, grammar, pronunciation, punctuation, word roots, literary analysis, and critical thinking.
- Windows and Mac
- $19.95 a month

APPS TO IMPROVE LANGUAGE-BASED READING DEFICITS

abc PocketPhonics
by Apps in My Pocket
http://www.appsinmypocket.com
- Apple app
- Designed to help young children use a phonics approach to learn letter sounds, practice writing letters, and learn to read 170 words.
- This app visually shows how to write each letter and then users can trace the letters with their finger or a stylus.
- Parents and teachers can adjust the level of accuracy needed for the tracing to avoid frustration, choose the way words are presented

(e.g., lowercase, uppercase, or cursive), and select from one of two popular handwriting styles.

- $1.99

Free Audio Books
by Spreadsong, Inc.
http://www.freeaudiobooksapp.com

- Apple app
- Many classic (2,947 at the time of this writing) audiobooks are available. The books are in the public domain and are read aloud by volunteers from Librivox.
- After selecting the book, the first chapter is sent immediately and chapters continue to be sent as the book is played unless the user specifies that he wants the entire book downloaded at once.
- Internet access is only needed during the downloading process.
- Related books are suggested while browsing and a 30-second rewind is available.
- $1.99

Free Books
by Spreadsong, Inc.
http://freebooksapp.com

- Apple app
- This iPad app helps users download 23,469 classic books that can be read with a built-in eReader.
- Automatic bookmarking saves the reader's place in a book.
- Users can browse books, view related books, and easily view other books by an author.
- $1.99

iAnnotate for iPad
by Aji
http://www.ajidev.com/iannotate

- Apple app
- This PDF reader empowers users to mark up the file to help with reading.
- Readers can highlight text, write notes, draw pictures, use stamps, underline, and create bookmarks for future reference.
- Users can type in any word to search for a document or part of a document and tabbed browsing facilitates reading more than one document at a time.

- PDFs can be transferred using e-mail, Dropbox, or iTunes.
- $9.99

iBooks
by Apple
http://www.apple.com/ipad/features/ibooks.html

- Apple app
- This app enables the iPad to be used as an eBook reader.
- It includes the iBookstore in which users can browse tens of thousands of books—many of them for free.
- After a book is downloaded, a tap will open it, swipes will turn pages, and pages can be bookmarked. Users can also type notes on pages that will be saved. It automatically saves the reading locations when the user exits and will indicate that place when the book is opened again on the same or another device with its automatic bookmark syncing feature.
- There are a variety of viewing options and the text, size, and font can be changed.
- Books can be viewed that include audio and video.
- A built-in dictionary appears when the user touches and holds down any word to look it up. The individual can also search for that word in the book or online.
- iBooks works with VoiceOver, the screen reader in iPad, so it can read the contents aloud of any page.
- Library books in the ePub electronic book format (and those that are Digital Rights Management or DRM-free) can be added to iTunes and synced to the device.
- Most PDF documents can be saved in iBooks.
- Free

Interactive Storybooks
- There are many interactive storybooks for the iPod touch, iPad, and Android systems that support literacy.
- The products encourage the user to watch, read, listen, and play as picture books come to life. Most use multitouch animation, painting, puzzles, games, hidden interactions, and top-quality graphics.
- Features may include multilevel games, a variety of page-turning modes, bookmark capabilities, picture/word association, professional narration, and options to customize the highlighting and reading aloud capabilities.
- Here are some Apple apps to try that typically cost less than $4.00:

o Jack and the Beanstalk Children's Interactive Storybook by Ayars Animation Inc

o Toy Story 2 Read-Along by Disney Publishing Worldwide Applications

o Dr. Seuss's ABC by Oceanhouse Media

Question Builder

by Mobile Education Tools

http://www.mobile-educationstore.com

- Apple app
- This app is designed to help elementary-aged children learn to answer questions.
- There are three levels of abstraction; settings can be configured to work on Why, Where, How, What, or Random question formats; and text and audio reinforcement can be turned on or off.
- To select an answer, the user selects the correct sentence on a dial.
- Progress is tracked on the app.
- $3.99

SuperWhy!

by PBS Kids

http://www.pbskids.org/superwhy

- Kids play games to promote learning to read and the use of alphabet skills, rhyming, spelling, comprehension, and vocabulary.
- The app includes engaging characters and animation for children.
- $2.99

VoiceOver

by Apple

http://www.apple.com/accessibility/voiceover

- The iPad comes with a screen reader and support for playback of closed-captioned content.
- It was developed as a gesture-based screen reader for the blind.
- When the feature is turned on in the settings menu, the reader touches the screen to hear a description, then double-taps, drags, or flicks to control the device.
- Triple clicking the home button turns VoiceOver on or off.
- VoiceOver speaks 18 languages and works with all of the applications built into the iPad.

WhQuestions
by Smarty Ears
http://www.smartyearsapps.com

- Apple app
- This app was developed to help children answer questions involving who, what, where, how, and why.
- The app provides 300 questions in a variety of formats that can be customized.
- Questions are provided in a written format and audio options are available to ask the questions aloud.
- A helper indicates if verbal responses are correct or incorrect.
- Users respond by tapping on the appropriate picture or verbalizing the response.
- Users slide a finger across the screen to proceed to the next question.
- Scores are saved to show progress.
- $9.99

Word Magic
by Anusen
http://www.anusen.com/iphone_word_magic.html

- Apple app
- This app uses colorful pictures with one letter missing from the printed word.
- There are three levels for children to use that involve choosing the missing letter at the beginning, middle, or end of a word.
- The pictures are amusing and children can shake the device to take them to the next word.
- $0.99

SOFTWARE FOR VISION-BASED READING DEFICITS

According to the National Center for Learning Disabilities (2010; http://www.ncld.org), a visual processing, or perceptual, disorder refers to a hindered ability to make sense of information taken in through the eyes. This is different from problems involving sight or sharpness of vision. Difficulties with visual processing affect how visual information is interpreted or processed by the brain. People with visual deficits often:

✓ reverse and invert letters,
✓ avoid reading,

✓ have difficulty copying written material,
✓ reread and skip lines,
✓ lose their place while reading,
✓ complain that print blurs while reading,
✓ turn their head while reading,
✓ hold their paper at odd angles to read,
✓ close one eye to read,
✓ have difficulty recognizing an object or word if only part of it is shown,
✓ misalign letters, and/or
✓ have messy papers.

People who have visual-perceptual deficits or low vision can often benefit from the use of text-to-speech or screen-reading software, which is described in the next section. Speed reading software may also be helpful for people with very subtle problems, but it is beyond the scope of this book.

Many programs highlight words and sentences as they are read aloud and work to help improve visual-perceptual skills. The highlighting can help with scanning and tracking the written words. In addition to the software described below, several nontechnological strategies can help improve reading. Low-tech strategies to help with visual-based deficits include using large-print books or a magnifying glass and providing tracking tools such as a ruler and lines.

Eye Track
by Tool Factory
http://www.toolfactory.com
- Eye Track is designed to train visual perception skills. Visual information is presented in a variety of ways to work on visual recognition, recall, discrimination, and meaning of visual input.
- This software is most appropriate for children.
- Windows and Mac
- $69.95

High Level Attention
by Learning Fundamentals
http://www.learningfundamentals.com
- This module is part of the Attention and Memory: Volume I CD and is available as a separate CD.

- One game on the CD is called Catch of the Day. Its goal is to improve visual scanning and identification as the complexity of the visual field increases. In this game, the user clicks on numbers embedded in a field of alphabet letters.
- This program may be used to train for compensatory strategies for hemianopsia and left-side neglect.
- There are 13 levels of difficulty.
- Windows and Mac
- $99.00

RedBar

by Bungalow Software

http://www.bungalowsoftware.com

- RedBar software helps individuals who have left or right neglect.
- At designated intervals, it trains users to notice (or attend to) their left or right side. If they don't click on the arrow that appears on the side of the screen that the client often ignores, RedBar gives them a stronger reminder.
- If they still fail to click the side, it shows a black arrow from within their intact visual field to guide them to the challenging side of the screen. The software works best when used in conjunction with another program, such as a word processor or while reading e-mail.
- Windows
- $79.50 for a single user; $50.00 a month as part of a subscription

SmartDriver

by BrainTrain

http://www.braintrain.com

- This program trains visual attention and perception, visual tracking, and self-control.
- It offers 90 progressive levels of difficulty with detailed record keeping.
- To win the game, the user needs to drive a car successfully through progressively more difficult roads and driving situations.
- Windows
- $309.00 for SmartDriver packaged with steering wheel with brake and accelerator pedals

CHAPTER 9

TREATMENT AND TECHNOLOGY TO IMPROVE WRITTEN EXPRESSION

People who have language and learning disabilities, strokes and head injuries, degenerative diseases, and other communication, cognitive, and physical challenges often have difficulty with one or more aspects of written language. As with other aspects of language and cognition, help from a trained education or rehabilitation professional should be used when possible to help select and implement the appropriate strategies and resources to facilitate progress.

Written expression is the final stage of literacy skill development. Difficulties experienced with listening, speaking, reading, and spelling can affect one's ability to express thoughts in print or writing.

There many skills that successful writers need to use:

✓ initiating writing activities;
✓ typing or writing by hand;
✓ maintaining attention to the task;
✓ retrieving words;
✓ sequencing the words into sentences;
✓ using proper grammar, syntax, and punctuation;
✓ spelling correctly; and
✓ organizing the written content.

To help children develop handwriting skills, a variety of positioning alternatives and low-tech options should be tried. Examples of low-tech options include alternative pens and pencils, pencil grips, slant boards, and special writing paper. There are also programs that have been developed such as Handwriting Without Tears (http://www.hwtears.com), which may be used to develop legible writing. There is quite a bit of research on the development of writing skills in children (see http://www.ldonline.org). A few online sources for low-tech options for improving written expression include http://www.onionmountaintech.com and http://www.theraproducts.com.

It is very important that children develop competent writing skills. The inability to express themselves in written form effectively can have far-reaching negative implications academically and in terms of self-esteem. There are also many experts who believe that learning cursive is important for brain development (see http://www.practical-parent.com/home/2010/1/29/cursive-and-brain-science.html for an overview and links to much of this research). If strategies and interventions to help the individual write well are not successful, it may be time to consider assistive technology to help with written expression and the physical act of putting words onto the paper. Students are growing up in an increasingly digitized world in which typing skills are becoming more important. Even if children do not have difficulties with handwriting, typing skills should be taught at a young age.

This chapter will discuss the following strategies and resources for improved writing:

- ✓ software and apps with customizable drill-and-practice exercises to improve writing,
- ✓ software and apps to improve spelling,
- ✓ features of word processors,
- ✓ text-based word processors,
- ✓ picture-based, talking word processors,
- ✓ word prediction programs,
- ✓ dictionaries,
- ✓ graphic organizers,
- ✓ technology to help with the physical aspect of writing and typing
- ✓ speech-to-text and voice recognition
- ✓ additional tools to help with written expression, and
- ✓ portable word processors, netbooks, and hybrids.

SOFTWARE AND APPS WITH CUSTOMIZABLE DRILL-AND-PRACTICE EXERCISES TO IMPROVE WRITING

There are quite a few programs patterned in a drill-and-practice format to improve writing skills. Such programs don't replace worksheets and workbook tasks, which still have value because typing and writing by hand are both valuable skills. However, the benefits of software use are many:

✓ Software for children help motivate and stimulate them to practice a variety of skills disguised through games and activities.

✓ Products for adults are typically more straightforward. These applications reinforce the need for repeated skills practice for people with writing difficulties.

✓ Quite a few programs are aimed at improving copying and generating words and sentences.

✓ There are programs targeted toward improving grammar, spelling, and punctuation.

✓ Many products on the market teach keyboarding skills.

✓ Programs vary in the options that are available for individualized practice.

✓ The same program with the same options may be used in different ways with different people to maximize the quality of each person's practice toward established goals.

✓ Correct responses are rewarded with a positive comment or graphic display.

✓ Incorrect responses are typically followed by guidance toward selecting the correct answer.

✓ If several incorrect responses are given by the user, it's best if the program provides assistance toward eliciting the correct response or provides a way to view the correct answer.

✓ Additional features of some drill-and-practice programs include a performance record, a main menu from which to select a variety of lessons, multiple-choice drills, and typing lessons in which the user is asked to type a correct word, letter, or sentence.

abc PocketPhonics
by Apps in My Pocket
http://www.appsinmypocket.com

- Apple app
- Designed to help young children use a phonics approach to learn letter sounds, practice writing letters, and learn to read the first 170 words.
- This app visually shows how to write each letter and then users can trace the letters with their finger or a stylus.
- Parents and teachers can adjust the level of accuracy needed for the tracing to avoid frustration, choose the way words are presented

(lowercase, uppercase, or cursive), and select from one of two popular handwriting styles.

- $1.99

Aphasia Tutor 1: Words +Out Loud and
Aphasia Tutor 2: Sentences +Out Loud
by Bungalow Software
http://www.bungalowsoftware.com

- These are customizable programs with many lessons of varying levels to improve written word retrieval skills and writing ability at the
letter, word, and sentence levels.
- The easiest tasks involve viewing a letter on the monitor and then
the user types it on the keyboard or finds a letter like it in a field
of four and selects it. More difficult tasks involve word retrieval
and spelling skills, but can be configured to provide assistance as
needed.
- Windows
- $149.50 for single user home version; $50.00 a month as part of a
subscription

Editor in Chief Software
by The Critical Thinking Co.
http://www.criticalthinking.com

- A variety of programs are available to help improve grammar, punc-
tuation, spelling, capitalization, and attention to detail.
- This software teaches the writer to analyze and edit stories that con-
tain errors in writing mechanics and story details.
- There are many different levels available for purchase.
- Windows and Mac
- $25.99

Essay Punch, Starter Paragraph Punch, Paragraph Punch,
Business Letter Punch, Writing for Business
by Merit Software
http://www.meritsoftware.com

- The Punch programs guide individuals through the process of writing an effective paragraph or essay. There are tutorials that respond
to typed material with personalized help and tips.
- Users select a topic and then use the programs' prewriting notepad
to collect relevant words and phrases. Working interactively with

the software, users develop an idea, create a topic sentence, compose the body of a paragraph or essay, and draft a conclusion.

- The Punch programs provide questions to guide users step-by-step through prewriting, organizing, writing, editing, and rewriting. Written works can be copied and pasted into other word processors or text editors.
- The programs work with the Internet Explorer, Firefox, and Safari browsers.
- $20.00 for a single user for 12 months (online versions); $69.00 for a single home user download

Grammar Fitness

by Merit Software

http://www.meritsoftware.com

- There are several programs in this series to help users of different ages master troublesome points of grammar.
- Lessons focus on correcting errors in punctuation, proper use of tenses, and identifying and correcting errors in usage.
- After an assessment, users advance through the program at their own pace. They receive personal help and feedback while they work.
- Five skill levels are available.
- The questions, answers, and explanations of the programs can be read aloud by the programs.
- Windows, Mac, and Linux
- $20.00 a month for 12 months for the online home version; $79.00 for each skill level for the CD

Grammar Jammers

by Pearson Education

http://pearsoned.com

- Apple app
- A number of different programs are available for students—primary, elementary, and middle.
- The apps use animations and games in their instruction and interactive questions to teach grammar.
- Topics include adjectives, adverbs, capitalizations, conjunctions, and more.
- Scores are tracked.
- The primary level app is free; the elementary and middle school apps are $2.99

GrammarPrep

by Pearson Education

http://www.pearsonhighered.com/grammarprep

- Apple app
- This is a grammar app made for college students and professionals.
- It includes multimedia tutorials, quizzes and tests, answer feedback, and progress tracking.
- Several apps are available focusing on different aspects of grammar such as apostrophes and using commas.
- $3.99

iWriteWords

by gdiplus

http://www.gdiplus.ptgdi.com

- Apple app
- This app was designed to teach children the proper way to write numbers and letters.
- The child slides a finger along while drawing the letters and then receives a rewarding animation.
- When finished with a word, the user tilts the device to watch the letters slide into a hold and advance to the next level.
- If playback is selected, the writer's own handwriting is shown.
- $2.99

KidsVoyager

by Innovism Software

http://kidsvoyager.com

- KidsVoyager is an online program to help kids learn to read and write.
- It uses a phonics reading and writing engine based on the premise that knowledge of initial and final sounds are among the first bits of language knowledge acquired.
- A subscription includes a consultation with a specialist as well as unlimited e-mail consultation about how to practice using the phonics engine during reading and writing exercises.
- Windows
- $285.00 for one year

No-Glamour Grammar Interactive Software

by Carolyn LoGuidice

http://www.linguisystems.com

- This program includes 600 items in interactive multisensory customizable lessons.
- There are activities covering 10 skill areas: comparitives, have/has, do/does, is/are, negatives, present tense, pronouns/possessives, questions (level 1), questions (level 2), regular/irregular past tense, and regular/irregular plurals.
- Progress is recorded and reports can be generated.
- Windows and Mac
- $43.95

No-Glamour® Question Structure Interactive Software

by Andrea M. Lazzari

http://www.linguisystems.com

- Two programs are available in this series: Interrogative Reversals and Wh- Questions
- Questions start with a narration and a picture. A second picture sequence (the pictures that correspond to the question) is shown 'and the user then drags each text box and releases it beneath its corresponding picture to formulate the question.
- The program has 9 units. Each unit has 13 questions that are arranged with increasing difficulty.
- Windows and Mac
- $43.95

Pictello

by AssistiveWare

http://www.assistiveware.com

- Apple app
- This app enables users to create talking books and photo albums on mobile devices.
- Stories can be created and edited using a Pictello wizard that guides the user through the process.
- Each page can contain a picture, up to five lines of text, recorded sounds, and high-quality text to speech.
- This app is a very motivating tool to encourage the development of written expression skills.
- $14.99

Punctuation Puzzler Software
by The Critical Thinking Co.
http://www.criticalthinking.com

- This program provides entertaining activities to practice using punctuation, grammar, usage, and reading comprehension for crystal clear communication.
- Users analyze context clues and apply punctuation rules to clarify the meaning of odd, convoluted, and misleading statements.
- Windows and Mac
- $21.99

Sentence Builder
by Mobile Education Tools
http://mobile-educationstore.com

- Apple app
- This program was designed to help users build grammatically correct sentences with a special emphasis on connector words.
- Users move from 1–5 words in a wheel so that they line up to create a sentence and match a picture.
- There are three levels of play with 100 pictures from which to create sentences. In Level 1, the subject and the adjective of each sentence is fixed so the user selects only the modifier and the verb. In Level 3, the student chooses the modifier, verb, and adjective. Progress is tracked.
- $3.99

Stories2Learn
by MDR
http://www.look2learn.com

- Apple app
- This app was developed to help children create personalized stories using their own voices, text, and pictures.
- Stories can be created by teachers, parents, and therapists to teach social skills or to teach steps in a task.
- Individuals who have difficulty with communication can create stories to assist with expression.
- $13.99

Story Patch
by Haywoodsoft
http://storypatch.com

- Apple app

- This is a story creator designed with the goal of helping kids create stories on their own or with the help of a template.
- The user first titles the story, then selects a theme such as "a trip to the zoo" or builds his story independently.
- If the templates are used, questions are presented with possible answers and the user selects her response to create a unique story.
- There is an image library with more than 800 images grouped into 47 categories to create settings for each page.
- A character designer or personal pictures can be used to create the characters in the story.
- $4.99

SOFTWARE TO IMPROVE SPELLING

The signs or symptoms of spelling problems may include, but are not limited to, the following examples:
- ✓ reversals and confusion of letters like b and d,
- ✓ omission of letters (called elisions),
- ✓ use of letters or syllables in the wrong order, and
- ✓ spelling words phonetically (how they sound).

Learning to spell correctly is a difficult task to master. If reading issues are present, the same underlying deficits that contribute to difficulty in reading also contribute to challenges with spelling. It is especially difficult when certain skills are weak such as:
- ✓ analyzing and recognizing the whole as being made up of individual parts,
- ✓ perceiving letter sounds and remembering them,
- ✓ decoding written words, and
- ✓ remembering sequences.

Many helpful suggestions for improving spelling can be found online at http://www.ldonline.org/article/5587 and http://www.ldonline.org/article/6192. There are also quite a few products developed primarily for spelling help. A quick search using the word "spelling" on Amazon.com will reveal a number of mainstream programs to improve spelling. There are also a few specialized programs created for people who may need to use switches or keyboards. Some of the programs that provide help with spelling during writing tasks will generate a list of misspelled works that can then be used in spelling lists to study. There are also a rapidly expanding number of spelling apps available and a review of all of them is beyond the scope of this book.

BigIQkids Spelling Program

by BigIQkids

http://SpellingTime.com

- This site offers programs for spelling as well as math, U.S. facts, and vocabulary.
- Users can register and log in to save information or just choose the quick play option.
- There is a choice to work on a customized spelling program, enter a spelling contest, or participate in a spelling bee.
- In the spelling program, a free online spelling tutor presents quizzes, spelling bees, spelling tests, and fun spelling games customized to each user's abilities.
- Spelling lists are available through the program or users can create a list of their own.
- Activities are created with the words and advanced based on performance.
- Words can be typed on a keyboard or a mouse can be used.
- Lessons can be printed.
- Free

Ghotit

http://www.ghotit.com

- This is a Microsoft Word spell checker add-in to help people who have writing challenges.
- It uses text-to-speech and takes into account the word's context and phonetic spelling.
- A dictionary is included.
- Versions are available for the U.S., U.K., Australia, and New Zealand.
- $99.00 for a lifetime subscription or $14.99 for 3 months

Ginger

by Ginger Software

http://www.gingersoftware.com

- Ginger was produced to help users with significant spelling and grammar errors.
- It helps with proofreading, grammar, and spelling using the full sentence context.
- It works with Microsoft Word, Outlook, PowerPoint, Internet Explorer, and Firefox and can be used online or offline.
- Ginger Premium offers text-to-speech and progress tracking.

- Writers can hear sentences before and after corrections and mistakes can be monitored to personalize instruction.
- Users can also listen to e-mails, websites, and documents in high-quality voices.
- Windows
- $99.00 or $9.90 a month for the premium version

Show Me Spelling
by Attainment Company
http://www.attainmentcompany.com
- Users can input a spelling list or work with lists that are provided.
- The 600 spelling words included have corresponding speech with pictures.
- Users spell by using the standard keyboard or on-screen alphabet.
- There is a hint option that will lightly flash the next letter in the word.
- When the "show me" button is pressed, the correct spelling goes across the screen.
- The program is single switch and IntelliKeys compatible.
- Windows and Mac
- $129.00

Spell-A-Word
by RJ Cooper & Associates
http://www.rjcooper.com
- This program uses large print and offers built-in scanning capabilities as well as feedback for blind users.
- It is a talking spelling and keyboarding software for beginning to advanced letter users.
- More than 1,000 words are included with real voice and picture groups.
- Groups can be manipulated in many ways (e.g., alphabetized, sorted, and scrambled) and exported for easy e-mailing and sharing.
- It enables parents and teachers to customize spelling lessons and incorporate spelling lists into the exercises.
- Voice prompts can be recorded and visual feedback can be used as needed. As words are learned, the verbal prompt becomes the main cue, and the visual cue fades.
- Windows and Mac
- $119.00

This Week's Words
by Simulant
http://www.thisweekswords.com

- Apple app
- This is a space-themed app that allows elementary-aged students to practice the words in their spelling lists. As new words are added, the old words move to a section of review words.
- Users first add their words, then play games to learn their words. There are three games to learn words involving different tasks—listening and choosing, completing a word, and spelling the word. The users then take practice tests.
- Parents or teachers should check the words to make sure that they are added correctly and children may take a little time getting used to the text-to-speech feature if words are pronounced incorrectly.
- The app accommodates multiple users.
- $2.99

Time4Learning
http://www.time4learning.com

- This program is an online interactive curriculum that teaches spelling primarily as a component within an overall language arts and phonics program.
- Time4Learning helps teach spelling by starting with the basics of hearing and recognizing the sounds (phonological and phonemic awareness) and then teaches the letters and sounds. Skills are built through spelling games and activities that teach blending, segmenting, word analysis, and fluency.
- The goal is for students to gain mastery of spelling and reading decoding skills simultaneously. Spelling lists of the sight words are taught through memorization techniques.
- $19.95 per month for one user

Vocabulary and SpellingCity.com
http://www.spellingcity.com

- This is an interactive online program designed to help individuals improve spelling skills and expand their vocabulary.
- Users can input a list of words or find a list sorted by grade and geographic location.
- In the testing mode, the user hears the word read aloud by a real voice. He clicks a button to hear the word again or another button to have the word used in a sentence. When the test is complete, the

student will see a screen with his grade on it. This screen allows the user to click "Teach Me" on the words he missed.

- There are a series of printable or online games using a customizable spelling word list. Individuals can enter 5–10 spelling words, and SpellingCity can turn this list into a word search, a matching game, HangMouse, crossword puzzle, or other activity.
- There are more than 43,000 words and sentences available for study.
- Users are able to log on to save lists.
- Free or $24.99 for five users in a premium membership

FEATURES OF WORD PROCESSORS

Text-based and picture-based word processors can greatly improve the quality of written work. The support provided with this type of software reduces physical effort and assists with organization so that writers are able to focus more on content. Both mainstream word processors and specialized assistive writing technology products offer a wide variety of helpful tools.

To select the most appropriate software for a particular individual, first determine which features will be most helpful to the writer. Also, consider price and the availability of training and continued support.

TEXT-BASED WORD PROCESSING FEATURES

Auditory feedback and text-to-speech. Auditory feedback and text-to-speech involve having the computer read text aloud after the user types a letter, word, sentence, or paragraph. When writers hear words or entire documents read aloud as they follow in the written text, their written expression improves. The auditory feedback also helps writers maintain attention to their tasks, catch mistakes early to avoid lengthy editing sessions later, and may even improve word selection.

Auto correct and abbreviation expansion. Auto correct and abbreviation expansion both correct commonly misspelled words and allow users to input abbreviations to be expanded when typed. For instance, if the user types "IST," the software could be programmed to expand it and type "Innovative Speech Therapy." Users can create frequently used words, phrases, or other standard pieces of text, saving keystrokes and time.

Dictionary and thesaurus. Many dictionaries can be customized and allow grammar checks tailored to the user's needs. Some programs read selections aloud, while others offer assistance by "thinking of words" for users with word retrieval challenges.

Editing. All word processing programs have methods of copying, cutting, and pasting, and formatting the presentation of the document. Some programs, such as Microsoft Word, enable users to see the changes that others make to their documents. The writer can decide whether to reject or accept the changes.

Online access and collaborative tools. There are now many online word processing programs that empower users to write online so that the content can be accessed from any online computer. Google Documents and the Office 2010 web apps enable users to work "in the cloud." These tools generally are quite convenient because the user is not tied to one computer and can more easily share documents with others.

Organization and outlining. Organizing software can help people who have difficulty getting started on and organizing written projects. Many of these programs offer the user the ability to outline narrative prior to writing the document. Some of the programs do so in a linear form; others use more of a brainstorming technique with webs. Each entry contains an idea, a concept, or a question that is visually linked together by branches to show their relationship to each other. Ideas don't have to be immediately formed into sentences. The user can have access to pictures, spell checkers, and text-to-speech. Brainstorming results can be converted into an outline and then edited to a finished product.

Picture or graphics support. Many individuals with communication and cognitive deficits are unable to read and write words. Pictures help improve written expression. Communication devices enable users to express themselves by clicking on pictures to generate written messages. Some software, quite a few Apple apps, and many dedicated communication devices on the market offer dynamic display. The user is initially presented with a set of pictures. Once an item is selected, more choices open up on the screen until the user finds the desired picture.

Speech/voice recognition. With speech- or voice-recognition software and computer hardware, a user trains the computer to recognize his or her voice for writing or giving computer commands. This process can be used to write within a word processor or to create an e-mail message. Typically, the more the system is used, the better able it is to understand what the user is saying. Incorrect words need to be corrected by either voice or keyboard commands in order to train the program for increased accuracy. Speech recognition provides potential hurdles for people with disabilities—especially those with intact cognitive and communication skills who have a visual or physical deficit that prevents them from being able to type well. As future technological advances occur, speech recognition technology should become a more effective solution for clients with communication and cognitive issues. Products are becoming increasingly affordable, require less initial training, and are easier to use.

Spelling and grammar assistance. Different word processors offer diverse types of spelling and grammar guidance. Some are equipped to help typists who can produce phonetic approximations of words. Other programs tailor the type of grammar to be focused on during the grammar check.

Study skills assistance. Almost all word processing programs offer the ability to highlight text. Some also enable the user to extract the highlighted material into a separate file for studying. Easy access to bookmarking, note-taking, summarizing, paraphrasing, and a dictionary are helpful study skill features of some word processors. By using the "find" feature, users can search for individual bookmarks and highlights. Text notes are helpful for visual processors, aiding the user to revisit and study important material. Using voice notes, users can dictate information such as oral summarizing and paraphrasing.

Visual presentation. Most word processing programs enable the user to change the background, text color, font, and size to promote increased comprehension and retention of material.

Web access with visual and auditory support. Several of the more advanced programs offer the ability to highlight, read aloud, and extract information from the web to other files.

Word prediction. Word prediction helps with many aspects of written literacy skills such as word retrieval, spelling, and sentence formation. This type of software can improve the user's attention span, confidence, independence, and language development. It may minimize the number of keystrokes for those with physical difficulty typing. The use of grammatical word prediction has been shown to improve the sentence structure and grammatical accuracy of text. Programs vary in the prediction methods used. Many advanced word processing programs offer the user a list of words after a letter has been typed or selected, based on previous words used. Some provide word lists based on spelling and frequency of word usage in prior documents and phonetic approximations of words that are written. Some programs enable the user to select the way the words are shown to the typist and the number of words to be included in the list. Keep in mind that in some instances word prediction programs may actually interfere with the writing process. The word list may be distracting and having to stop and choose words may slow down some writers.

TEXT-BASED WORD PROCESSORS

Word processing software and assistive writing products assist with the speed and effectiveness of the writing process. They differ in the features included, the level of assistive support they provide, the way they are presented, and the cost. Some products include written materials for the educator, as well as downloadable lessons with particular subject content that correlates with the school curriculum.

Begin by selecting the most important features, then try a few products with those features. Sometimes the more features that are available, the better the product; in other situations, the simpler the product, the better.

There are products that work within their own word processing systems and others that work in Microsoft Word or with other formats such as e-mail or the Internet. A few products are used more in the elementary and middle school years, because they offer supportive materials that are an integral part of school curriculum. Others are geared to higher level students and people in the working world.

Co:Writer 6

by Don Johnston

http://www.donjohnston.com

- Co:Writer works in conjunction with multiple word processing and Internet applications, including e-mail. As words are typed, it interprets spelling and grammar mistakes and offers word suggestions immediately.
- This product is widely used in school systems to enhance many aspects of literacy.
- Windows and Mac
- $325.00

Google Docs

http://www.docs.google.com

- Google Docs offers cloud-based document editing and storage.
- It is ideal for working on writing documents when a group of people need to make changes to a document or a person desires to access documents from multiple computers.
- Real-time coediting is available so more than one person can edit a document at the same time. It offers automatic file saving with easy access to earlier versions and it exports and imports most standard formats.
- There is no need to install software on your computer.

- The documents can be viewed in all mobile browsers such as those on Android devices and iPhones.
- There is built-in optical character recognition so that users can upload and convert PDF or image files into text.
- Chat options are available so that users can talk to each other as edits are made.

iWork '09
by Apple
http://www.apple.com/iwork

- iWork '09 includes Pages (like Word), Numbers (like Excel), and Keynote (like PowerPoint). The functions included in Entourage are provided by Mail, Address Book, and iCal.
- Pages is a streamlined word processor and an easy-to-use page layout tool.
- Helpful features include: spell checking, proofreading, generation of table of contents, viewing document in full screen to get rid of clutter, ability to organize ideas in outline mode and expand or collapse topics and drag and drop them where needed, change tracking to keep track of edits, option to view thumbnails of pages or sections, and it can open Word files or save Pages documents as Word files or PDFs.
- Here is a great site with tutorials: http://www.apple.com/iwork/tutorials.
- Mac
- $79.00

Kurzweil 3000
by Kurzweil Educational Systems
http://www.kurzweiledu.com

- Kurzweil 3000 is a comprehensive reading, writing, and learning software solution for struggling writers.
- Delivery models include stand alone, network, web license, and USB.
- This program reads aloud electronic or scanned text and provides support for writing and studying with active learning, studying, and test-taking strategies.
- There is a multilanguage recognition option.
- A picture dictionary is included with more than 1,300 graphics in English and Spanish.

- The program includes enhanced writing supports like a Start Writing button, Write menu, writing templates, Create Draft button, Review button, and word underlining for spelling.
- Windows and Mac
- Kurzweil 3000 Read/Scan Color with Classic Literature CD—$1,495

Microsoft Word 2007
by Microsoft Corporation
http://www.microsoft.com

- Microsoft Word is the standard word processing software program in both the educational world and the business world.
- Word includes many learning and accessibility features of which most users are unaware. Many features in this program can help people who are struggling with reading and writing. When used in conjunction with more specialized software, it can be even more effective in helping people with a wide variety of reading and writing challenges. More information on Word's accessibility options can be found at http://www.microsoft.com/Office/system/accessibility.
- Word's spell checker falls rather short for people who have difficulty recognizing words, such as people with aphasia or visual perceptual deficits. They may struggle to read the suggestions, and without any definitions they may not understand what the words mean. Also, this program can only cope with fairly basic spelling errors, such as missing and additional letters, and very common phonetic errors.
- There are features included in Microsoft Word that will help the writer with the following tasks: generating summaries, highlighting text, checking spelling, adjusting the grammar checkers, checking the readability of selected text, linking highlighted words to dictionary definitions and a thesaurus, using abbreviation expansion, adjusting character and line spacing, decluttering the toolbar, accessing the toolbar with the keyboard, creating templates for writing or note-taking, creating text boxes and shapes for quick graphic organizers, inserting audio or text comments, changing the visual presentation of the text, inserting graphics, and zooming into a portion of the page.
- Word also allows users to auto summarize, auto complete, and auto correct.
- It provides both text-to-speech and speech-to-text capabilities.
- A Spanish version is available.
- Windows and Mac
- $149.99 (Student and Teacher bundle)

Microsoft Word 2010

http://www.microsoft.com/enable/products/office2010

- The 2010 version offers the features of Word 2007 except for the ability to summarize written material.
- Users can collaborate online with web apps.
- This version allows users to point to a word or selected phrase with the mouse and a translation displays in a small window. It also provides for pronunciation of the word and copying and pasting of the translation.
- It has speech recognition capabilities.
- Users can add alternative text descriptions to shapes, pictures, tables, and graphics.
- The accessibility checker tool will identify areas that might be challenging for users with disabilities to view or use, and by providing a task pane to review those areas, users can fix potential problems with their content.
- Windows and Mac
- $149.99 (Home and Student bundle); $279.99 (Home and Business bundle); $499.99 (Professional Academic bundle, available through authorized academic resellers only)

MyStudyBar

by JISC Regional Support Centres

http://www.rsc-ne-scotland.ac.uk/eduapps/mystudybar.php

- This is a comprehensive set of portable open source and freeware applications to support learners with literacy difficulties.
- It uses a floating toolbar to support literacy.
- Speech recognition only works in Vista or Windows 7.
- The toolbar includes a range of tools to support inclusion such as mind mapping, screen masking, word prediction, talking dictionary, and text-to-speech capabilities.
- Text can be saved as MP3 files.
- Windows
- Free

OpenOffice.org 3

by Oracle

http://www.openoffice.org

- This site is available in multiple languages.
- Users can read, edit, and save to Microsoft Word, Microsoft Excel, and Microsoft PowerPoint file formats and import and edit PDF files.

- Windows, Mac, Linux, and the Oracle Solaris operating system
- Free

Read&Write GOLD

by Texthelp Systems

http://www.texthelp.com

- A customizable toolbar seamlessly integrates with familiar applications including Microsoft Word, Internet Explorer, and Adobe Reader, allowing users to access the support tools they need from within mainstream software programs.
- It highlights and reads text aloud using natural sounding voices and also includes a comprehensive set of support tools for reading, writing, studying, research, and test taking.
- The program's benefits for writing include: translator, phonetic spell checker based on the user's spelling patterns, homophone checker, word prediction that learns the user's vocabulary patterns, a talking dictionary, web highlighting, DAISY reader for those who are print disabled, Word Wizard (thesaurus), scanning function, screenshot reader, screen masking to block out text or spotlight paragraphs and sentences, study skills toolbar, calculator, text-to-speech capabilities on documents and PDFs, and research tools (fact finder, fact folder, and fact mapper).
- Windows and Mac
- $645.00

Solo 6 Literacy Suite

by Don Johnston

http://www.donjohnston.com

- The Solo 6 Literacy Suite includes four programs: Co:Writer, Write: OutLoud, Draft:Builder, and Read:OutLoud.
- Co:Writer adds word prediction, grammar, and vocabulary support capabilities to any word processor or e-mail program. It opens up as a separate screen on the monitor and helps with spelling, composition, and revision. Struggling writers who use phonetic spelling benefit from FlexSpell. WordBanks and topic dictionaries give targeted vocabulary support.
- Write:OutLoud is a talking word processing program that uses purposeful revision and editing tools to help writers make changes and improve their writing.
- Draft:Builder guides students to develop a strategic approach to planning, organizing, and writing drafts. Students add concepts and

ideas to an outline and a visual map is automatically created. They can then change the order and outline level and then add notes and assign them to an outline point. Students drag notes from the outline and drop them into a draft area and then add more sentences and work on grammar.

- Read:OutLoud is a text reader that reads aloud and highlights all common electronic file formats. Clicking on the web tab allows students to browse and save web pages into their document or work file. Supported reading guides are provided to remind students of effective strategies. eHighlighters can capture important information. The bibliographer helps students create a bibliography. A dictionary is located in the toolbar.
- Windows and Mac
- $839.00

Talking Word Processor

by Premier Literacy

http://www.readingmadeeasy.com

- Talking Word Processor is an easy-to-use, fully functional word processor with text-to-speech capability.
- It is compatible with all standard word processor files.
- It includes features such as word prediction, talking grammar checker, Language Model Information Summarization (LMIS), a 250,000-word integrated dictionary, and highlighting and extraction tools.
- Windows
- $99.95

WordQ 3

by Quillsoft

http://www.wordq.com

- WordQ is a software tool that can be used along with standard writing software.
- It uses word prediction, highlighting, and auditory feedback to assist with typing and proofreading.
- When the user has completed typing a sentence, text-to-speech capabilities enable the text to be read aloud.
- The program can also be set up to read letters and words or entire documents aloud.
- WordQ internally spell checks words for prediction purposes, but does not replace the spell checker. It enhances the user's spelling and grammar through its intelligent word prediction and speech

feedback features, such as allowing the user to hear spelling suggestions made by Microsoft Word.
- Windows and Mac
- $199.00

Write:OutLoud 6

by Don Johnston
http://www.donjohnston.com
- Write:OutLoud is a talking word processing program that uses purposeful revision and editing tools to help writers make changes and
improve their writing.
- Windows and Mac
- $107.00

WriteOnline

by Crick Software
http://www.cricksoft.com/us/products/WriteOnline/default.htm
- This product resembles other word processors, but works online.
- It includes auditory support, word banks, word prediction, and
writing frames.
- WriteOnline also includes phonetic word prediction, the ability to
caption pictures, speech options, and vision enhancements for all
toolbars and menus.
- As with most Crick Software, the purchase of this products allows
teachers and parents access to http://www.learninggrids.com—
Crick's site for sharing resources, including ready-made toolbars.
- $200 (single-user, one-year subscription)

WYNN Wizard

by Freedom Scientific
http://www.freedomscientific.com/LSG
- WYNN uses four color-coded rotating toolbars.
- There are many supports for the writing process:
  o The toolbars emphasize file management, visual and auditory
  presentation of text, traditional study tools, writing aids, and
  Internet use.
  o Full editing capabilities are provided, including the ability
  to modify electronic files, scanned pages, or newly created
  documents.
  o Special dictionaries, a thesaurus, a homophone checker, word
  prediction, highlighters, outline tools, voice notes, and text
  notes provide features to support individual learning styles.

o   Users can highlight text directly on a web page and extract the text into a WYNN document.

- It is compatible with WebCT—an online proprietary virtual learning environment system.
- Windows
- $995.00

WYNN Reader
by Freedom Scientific
http://www.freedomscientific.com/LSG
- WYNN Reader includes all the features available in WYNN Wizard (described above) with the exception of OCR (or scanning) capability and the ability to open PDF files.
- Windows
- $375.00

PICTURE-BASED, TALKING WORD PROCESSORS

People with severe reading and writing deficits who are unable to use text-based word processors to write are often able to benefit from picture-based, talking word processors. These programs typically offer speech feedback, symbols or pictures to support text, and on-screen grids for writing and communication. Users create written documents by either typing directly into the word processor or by clicking on-screen grids that contain symbols, words, or letters. These programs enable the therapist or parent to create writing activities specifically suited to individuals, incorporating as much or as little picture and sound support as needed.

Clicker 5
by Crick Software
http://www.cricksoft.com/us/products/clicker
- Clicker is a powerful and easy-to-use writing and reading support and multimedia tool that can be used with a wide variety of clients.
- It enables the user to write with whole words, phrases, or pictures.
- Users can hear words in the Clicker Grid before writing or to proofread after writing. The words are highlighted as they are spoken.

- This switch-accessible software has customizable grids on the bottom half of the screen in which words and pictures are located and to which pop-up grids can be added. There is a grid-editing toolbar. Available templates include "phrases," in which an entire phrase is placed in a cell.
- Many sentence-building grids, templates for talking books, and an extensive picture library are available.
- Animation, digital recordings, a variety of software voices, and video can be used.
- Clicker includes a range of extensive accessibility options for students with low vision.
- Many curriculum-based activities are available for download.
- Windows and Mac
- $249.00 for single user

Communicate:SymWriter
by DynaVox Mayer-Johnson
http://www.mayerjohnson.com

- Communicate:SymWriter is a talking word processor that uses symbols to help learners of all ages and abilities read and write.
- The startup launcher of Communicate:SymWriter opens with four color-coded interface levels to enhance writing fluency for beginning and more advanced writers.
- The program features more than 9,000 Picture Communication Symbols (PCS) and more than 8,000 Widgit Literacy Symbols (WLS).
- It automatically converts parts of speech into grammatically appropriate symbols while typing the document, and it reduces the need for manual corrections.
- Communicate:SymWriter provides the perfect tool for simple word and symbol processing for emergent writers. It enables users to see the meaning of words as they write. The symbols appear automatically in a side panel, illustrating the word just typed or chosen. Non-keyboard users can write in very flexible ways by selecting from grids and buttons.
- Clipart, symbols, or imported images can be easily dropped onto the page to add further visual support.
- Windows
- $229.00

PixWriter

by Slater Software

http://www.slatersoftware.com

- This software provides a picture-rich environment for reading and writing.
- It includes more than 10,500 Literacy Support Pictures in both black-and-white and color versions. Digital images can also be added.
- When the user selects a button, the word and picture appear and the computer speaks.
- There are options for 16, 36, and 64 button setups.
- The voice, rate, and pronunciation can be customized.
- This program provides picture-assisted writing so that writers can use whole words and sentences.
- Write with mouse, keyboard, touch screen, one and two-step switch scanning, joystick, and whiteboard.
- Documents can be saved, and alternate modes of access, such as single-switch scanning and adapted keyboards, can be used.
- Windows and Mac
- $199.00 for single user

WordPower and Picture WordPower

by Inman Innovations

http://www.inmaninnovations.com

- WordPower is a word-based vocabulary design that combines features of a core vocabulary, spelling, and word prediction. The core words are color-coded and categorized for easy access.
- The user selects words to form messages that are read aloud by the computer.
- Picture WordPower consists of single hit words, category-based words, and spelling with word prediction.

Word Prediction Programs

The inability to recall words while writing significantly impedes the writing process. Word prediction software, apps, and other specialized tools can be used to improve spelling, broaden vocabulary, speed up the typing process, and boost the confidence of writers. Specialized dictionaries can also be helpful for individuals with word retrieval issues. They offer a number of ways to help the writer think of words by following a series of links to related words.

Assistive Chat
by Assistive Apps
http://www.assistiveapps.com
- Apple app
- This app was developed to speed up the typing for people who are unable to communicate verbally.
- Word prediction minimizes the number of keystrokes needed.
- The program's ability to predict words improves with use.
- Frequently used sentences and phrases can be saved.
- Recently used sentences can be accessed.
- $24.99

Premier Predictor Pro
by Premier Literacy
http://www.readingmadeez.com/products/PredictorPro.html
- "P3" is a talking word prediction program that works with programs on the computer that require typing such as e-mail, word processing, and spreadsheets.
- Frequency of use, sentence content, frequently misspelled words, recent words, and words that may be added to a dictionary are all used to generate the predicted word list.
- Power search is included to help users search when they only know part of the word.
- This program supports English, French, and Spanish and offers many occupation-specific word libraries.
- P3 can be purchased individually or bundled with other programs by Premier Literacy.
- Windows
- $89.95

SoothSayer Word Prediction
by Applied Human Factors Inc.
http://www.ahf-net.com/sooth.htm
- SoothSayer Word Prediction is a software program that works in conjunction with other programs, such as word processors, web browsers, databases, and spreadsheets.

- In addition to word prediction, it offers text-to-speech, abbreviation expansion, and sentence completion with text up to 500 characters long.
- It comes with a built-in dictionary of more than 11,000 words that can be customized and offers more than 350 frequently used sentences based on abbreviation expansion that can be customized.
- Windows
- $149.00

Typ-O
by SecondGuess
http://typ-o.com
- Apple app
- This app uses a word prediction engine and spelling error model to help people write more accurately.
- Text-to-speech helps writers listen to words prior to selecting them.
- Text can be e-mailed or pasted into other applications.
- This app does not detect errors in grammar or syntax.
- $5.99 for iPhone; $9.99 for iPad

DICTIONARIES

There are quite a few free online dictionaries, including:
- ✓ **Dictionary.com**: http://www.dictionary.com
- ✓ **The Free Dictionary**: http://www.thefreedictionary.com
- ✓ **Merriam-Webster**: http://www.merriam-webster.com
- ✓ **Merriam-Webster's Word Central**: http://www.wordcentral.com
- ✓ **YourDictionary.com**: http://www.yourdictionary.com

People with word retrieval and spelling challenges can often benefit from dictionaries that help them find target words when they can only type a part of the word or a related word.

Shahi
by Abdullah Arif
http://blachan.com/shahi
- Shahi is a visual dictionary that combines Wiktionary content that includes a definition and examples of word use in a sentence with

images from Flickr, Google, and Yahoo that correlate with the specified word.

- Users type the word and pick the image feed.
- Free

Visuwords
by The Logical Octopus
http://www.visuwords.com

- This is an online graphic dictionary and thesaurus.
- Users can look up words to find their meanings and connections to other words.
- The color and pattern of the links between words show their relationships and the connections can be moved to clarify meanings.
- Free

WordWeb Pro 6
by WordWeb Software
http://wordweb.info

- Once installed, WordWeb can be activated from almost any Windows program by holding down the Ctrl key and clicking on the word to look up words, find synonyms, or suggest related words.
- It includes 70,000+ pronunciations, 4,900 usage examples, and has helpful spelling and sounds-like links. Additional word lists can be purchased.
- Windows
- $19.00 for single user

GRAPHIC ORGANIZERS: TECHNOLOGY FOR ORGANIZING WRITTEN NARRATIVE

For many people with writing challenges, one of the most difficult steps of the writing process is getting started. Recording thoughts in a clear and logical way is often difficult. Outlining, semantic webbing, graphic organizing, and visually based study software create visual-graphic support, help organize ideas, and can assist with converting those visual maps into outlines. To learn more about mind mapping and the many available options, visit Brian Friedlander's blog at http://assistivetek.blogspot.com.

Several programs are helpful to writers who need assistance with developing ideas, organizing, outlining, and brainstorming. Using images or graphs can help people with reading and writing challenges understand abstract concepts in a concrete way. Graphics combined with text can facilitate learning better than text alone. Software such as Inspiration allows users to input text or pictures in smaller segments and slowly build them into a finished document. Microsoft Word and PowerPoint can assist with organizing documents. By using outlining software and graphic organizers, writers are often more easily able to sequence and expand their writing.

Inspiration 9
by Inspiration Software
http://www.inspiration.com/Inspiration

- This software has become mainstream in many school systems and is ideal for visual mapping, outlining, writing, and making presentations.
- It was produced with students in grades 6–12 in mind, but is also appropriate for adults.
- In Diagram View, users can brainstorm and capture ideas quickly; show relationships with links; use symbols to represent their ideas visually; differentiate ideas with colors, shapes, patterns, shadows, fonts, and styles; and instantly arrange the diagram into different tree charts.
- In Map View, users can expand the mind map by adding a new topic and subtopic branches that can be rearranged and dragged to new places and use the Relationship tool to show connections among branches and topics.
- In Outline View, users can capture ideas and information and add topics at different levels with single commands, transform notes and paragraphs into individual topics to reorganize information, hide and show levels of detail, and transfer the outline to word processor programs.
- The included Presentation Manager allows students to create presentations from their Diagram, Map, or Outline View screens and add additional graphics, video, and sound.
- Windows and Mac
- $69.00 for a single user on a desktop computer

Kidspiration 3
by Inspiration Software
http://www.inspiration.com/Kidspiration

- With this junior version of Inspiration for grades K–5, users build graphic organizers by combining pictures, text, and spoken words to represent thoughts and information.

- There is a Symbol Maker drawing tool, many SuperGrouper images, and symbols paired with words in the Writing View.
- Users can add speech support by choosing to use the Listen tool.
- In Picture View, students develop thought webs and other graphic organizers.
- In Writing View, they expand their ideas into written expression.
- The Kidspiration Word Guide provides access to definitions, recorded speech for pronunciation, synonyms and antonyms, parts of speech, and sample sentences for nearly 13,000 words.
- Windows and Mac
- $69.00 for a single user on a desktop computer

RecallPlus Study Software
by RecallPlus
http://www.recallplus.com

- This software encourages users to write down the information that they need to learn visually on a card and to link the content visually using concept maps.
- Verbal information about the card can be recorded, as hearing the information can enhance learning and memory. Images can be obtained from an image library.
- This program tracks learned information and assists the person studying in focusing on weaker areas.
- Windows
- There is a RecallPlus Lite version that is free and can be used to visually represent notes. Paid versions are available to assist with testing knowledge of the information.
- $49.95 for the Essentials Edition; $69.95 for the Professional Edition; $99.95 for the Expert Edition

ONLINE GRAPHIC ORGANIZERS

Mindomo
by Expert Software Applications
http://www.mindomo.com

- Mindomo is collaborative mind mapping and brainstorming software to encourage free thinking and creativity.
- The interface is easy-to-use and offers multiple options for attaching multimedia and creating visual maps that can be exported in a PDF format or image file.
- Free and paid plans are available

Webspiration

by Inspiration Software

http://www.mywebspiration.com

- This is an online visual thinking, learning, and collaboration tool produced primarily with students in mind.
- It can be used individually or shared for collaboration.
- It is accessible with screen readers and supported by almost all web browsers.
- Users can brainstorm ideas, visualize concepts, organize information, and collaborate with others.
- Work is automatically saved and stored online.
- Collaborators create, edit, and comment on the same document.
- The Diagram View allows users to create bubble diagrams, flow charts, concept maps, process flows, and other visual representations of their thoughts.
- The Outline View helps users take notes, organize their work, and expand on their ideas.
- Users can sign up for a free beta test subscription.

TECHNOLOGY TO HELP WITH THE PHYSICAL ASPECT OF WRITING AND TYPING

The physical act of writing is problematic for many people who have fine motor coordination problems and weakness in their upper extremities. Those with mild physical difficulties may benefit from the accessibility options included with Microsoft Windows and Macintosh OS X.

ALTERNATIVE INPUT DEVICES

Writers with severe physical difficulties may benefit from alternative input devices. These may include, but are not limited to, adaptive keyboards, key guards, switches, touch screens, head-operated and eye-gaze pointing devices, Morse code input devices, brain-actuated pointing devices, voice input systems, speech-to-text software, voice-recognition or voice-command software, and cursor enlargement software.

KEYBOARD OPTIONS

Most operating systems offer options to make keyboards easier to use if the user has a tremor, has limited vision, or can only use one hand. Here are some accommodations offered for Windows users:

✓ **StickyKeys:** When turned on, StickyKeys allows users to press keys simultaneously that would normally take two hands. For example, it lets you hold down the CTRL key first and then ALT and then DEL and the computer will "hold" all three down in succession for you.

✓ **Filter Keys:** This control allows users with tremors or accidental extra keystrokes to type without the keyboard picking up the second hit.

✓ **ToggleKeys:** For those with visual impairments, when ToggleKeys is on, a specific tone is played when CAPS, CAPS LOCK, NUMBER LOCK, or SCROLL LOCK are on.

ON-SCREEN KEYBOARDS

An on-screen keyboard displays a visual keyboard with all of the standard keys. You can select keys using the mouse or another pointing device, or you can use a single key or group of keys to cycle through the keys on the screen. There are many different designs of on-screen keyboards, each having their own specific features and functionality. Both Windows and Mac computers now come with built-in on-screen keyboards.

Click-N-Type
by Lake Software
http://www.lakefolks.org/cnt/#Download

- Click-N-Type is a free, fully featured, on-screen virtual keyboard designed for individuals who have difficulty typing on a physical computer keyboard. It is designed with special consideration for the severely handicapped.
- Features include: word prediction and completion, AutoClick and Scanning modes, many available language and keyboard packs, a keyboard designer, and many user-designed layouts and audible and visible feedback options including spoken keys.
- It is fully configurable and includes macros.
- Windows
- Free

KeyStrokes
http://www.assistiveware.com

- This is an advanced on-screen keyboard for a Mac that allows users to type with a mouse, trackball, head pointer, or other mouse emulator.

- It offers advanced multilingual word prediction.
- The LayoutKitchen allows users to design their own virtual keyboards, not only for typing, but also to launch applications, speak, run AppleScripts, and much more.
- It provides powerful shortcut expansion features.
- Mac
- $299.00

TYPING

There are many software programs that assist with typing. A comprehensive review of the many types of products available is beyond the scope of this guide. There are also a few free online programs. A few websites for reviewing typing software are:

✓ **SuperKids Educational Software Review**: http://www.superkids.com/aweb/pages/reviews/typing

✓ **TopTenREVIEWS**: http://typing-software-review.toptenreviews.com

Custom Typing Training
by Custom Solutions
http://www.customtyping.com

- The keyboarding instruction can be customized to provide verbal coach-presented lessons for simple step-by-step keyboarding training.
- The keyboard graphics are very big, bright, and bold, so it is very clear about which finger to use for each key.
- There are more than 1,000 built-in exercises and others can be created.
- A keyboarding goalie soccer game can run at very slow levels, so that almost any student, no matter how slow, can play the game.
- For users who are evaluating alternate input systems and/or specialized hardware and software, Custom Typing provides extensive tools to customize setup, which leads to the most rapid and accurate text entry.
- Everything runs from the user's web browser. There is no software to install.
- Windows and Mac
- $9.00 per month (individual subscription)

Type to Learn 4: Agents of Information
by Sunburst
http://www.sunburst.com

- This software provides typing instruction with more than 100 levels and activities while engaging in futuristic world activities.
- It emphasizes both accuracy and speed while using proper positioning with individualized remediation and goals.
- There is a teacher management area, Spanish support for ESL learning, and closed captioning and text support for those with hearing impairments.
- Lessons are targeted toward K–12 users with different user interfaces and levels for different grades. Each lesson focuses on five keyboarding skills: left and right hand coordination, words per minute speed, rhythm, use of the shift key, and accuracy.
- Windows and Mac
- $39.95 (or a web-enabled version for $89.95)

Dance Mat Typing
by BBC Schools
http://www.bbc.co.uk/typing

- This is an interactive flash-based typing tutorial that contains animated typing tutors.
- This entertaining program is aimed at children aged 7–11 years. It is divided into four levels, each with three stages. In each stage, two or more keys on the keyboard are introduced.
- Windows and Mac
- Free

SPEECH-TO-TEXT AND VOICE RECOGNITION

Several available programs will type the words that the user speaks into a microphone. The biggest advantage of voice-recognition software is the ability to do hands-free computing, which is very helpful for people with limited mobility or a disability with written expression. Most require that the program be "trained" to the user's word pronunciation and speech style. Most of these programs require a substantial cognitive load. This is often an effective method for assisting users to quickly get thoughts recorded as text, but it requires considerable practice to use efficiently. This type of software is often difficult for people who have communication and cognitive deficits. However, a program called SpeakQ by Quillsoft, described below, offers a potential solution for these clients. Also, apps are available for portable devices that require less training. For a review of the mainstream products, please take a look at http://voice-recognition-software-review.toptenreviews.com.

iDictate
http://www.iDictate.com
- This is a service that enables the user to dictate a document using a telephone, Blackberry, or dictation device, and then receive the completed job back for editing via e-mail within a day.
- The cost for general dictation varies on a per word pricing structure.

Dragon Mobile Apps
by Nuance
http://www.nuance.com/dragonmobileapps
- Dragon Mobile Apps enable users of BlackBerry, iPad, iPhone, and iPod touch devices to use their voice for entering text.
- Multiple languages are supported.
- The Internet is required.
- Free

Dragon NaturallySpeaking (for PC)
by Nuance
http://www.nuance.com
- NaturallySpeaking is a voice-recognition program that allows the user to use continuous or natural speech patterns to enter data and execute commands.
- The user can dictate and edit directly into a computer or into a Nuance-certified handheld device. When synced with the PC, Dragon NaturallySpeaking can then transcribe the recorded dictation.
- This software can be difficult for users who have communication and cognitive challenges. All commands are given verbally.
- The program allows for web and computer searches.
- Bluetooth support
- $99.99 and up depending on version selected

WordQ + SpeakQ

by Quillsoft

http://www.goqsoftware.com

- WordQ + SpeakQ is designed specifically to help those who struggle with writing. It is a writing tool that enhances writing applications with fully integrated word prediction, spoken feedback, and speech recognition. Users can use a combination of dictation, word prediction, and typing to produce text.
- The training part of the program involves word repetition rather than reading aloud and offers words that are similar while you write to help improve vocabulary and variety.
- Abbreviations are expandable, so if the user says "my e-mail" it would write out his e-mail address.
- The program works in English, French, Spanish, and German.
- SpeakQ requires WordQ to work. It is an add-on.
- Windows
- $279.00

ADDITIONAL TOOLS TO HELP WITH WRITTEN EXPRESSION

Dial2Do Handsfree Assistant

by Dial2Do

http://www.dial2do.com

- Create reminders, send texts, listen to e-mail, and send e-mail from your phone.
- It uses a combination of technology and human quality control to transcribe your message.
- When necessary, human transcribers will listen to your audio recording.
- $2.49–$5.99 a month

Livescribe Echo Pen

by Livescribe

http://www.livescribe.com

- This pen records all that is said as the user writes. The recorded audio can be replayed by tapping directly on the special dot paper with the pen that recorded the audio.

- MyScript from Livescribe provides handwriting recognition so that the text can be converted to a Word document.
- Notes can be saved and searched for online or on a computer.
- Apps are available for games, reference guides, and productivity tools.
- Notes and recordings can be shared using the Pencast application. These recordings can be sent with an e-mail or embedded online.
- Creative users can use this pen to create talking flashcards, schedules, communication boards, and memory books by recording speech on the special paper and then cutting up the paper and putting them on index cards or in a scrapbook.
- 4 GB Echo Smartpen: $169.95 for 400 hours of audio (varies by audio quality setting)

PORTABLE WORD PROCESSORS, NETBOOKS, AND HYBRIDS

Portable word processors are generally lightweight and have instant on and off switches. The LED screen typically has anywhere from 6–8 lines of text when writing. Many of these devices can run on standard or rechargeable batteries for extended periods of time without having to recharge or change the batteries. Several portable note takers can be purchased with text-to-speech support and word prediction.

Netbooks usually weigh about 2 or 3 pounds and have an 8.9-inch diagonal LCD screen with a smaller keyboard than typically found on a notebook computer. They are intended for word processing and accessing the web. They ship with varying operating systems and memory. Many of the netbooks do not have a traditional hard drive. It is necessary to purchase a USB optical drive if you intend to install programs from a CD. Wi-Fi is typically built in. Microsoft Word with text-to-speech support may be the ideal writing tool for a student with a netbook. Devices offer varying levels of writing assistance, such as the use of a dictionary/thesaurus, word prediction, text reader, and spell checker. Storage capacity, keyboard layouts, and accessibility options vary.

- ✓ **NEO**: http://www.alphasmart.com
- ✓ **Writer and Fusion**: http://www.writerlearning.com
- ✓ **ASUS Eee PC**: http://eeepc.asus.com/us
- ✓ **Inspiron Mini 9**: http://www.dell.com
- ✓ **Aspire One**: http://www.acer.com
- ✓ **HP Mini Note**: http://www.hp.com

CHAPTER 10

TECHNOLOGY TO IMPROVE COGNITION, LEARNING, AND MEMORY

Cognitive impairments in memory, reasoning, attention, learning, judgment, and self-awareness are prominent roadblocks for functional independence and a productive lifestyle. Impaired cognition can be detrimental to rehabilitation and education efforts. The level of deficits can be severe or subtle. People with impaired cognition may display the following characteristics:

✓ reduced attention and difficulty concentrating during a task,
✓ inability to sequence and organize information,
✓ poor analytical skills and judgment,
✓ difficulty figuring out solutions to problems,
✓ a hard time learning and retaining new information,
✓ impaired ability to learn and remember names and events,
✓ inefficient time management skills,
✓ slow processing of new information,
✓ deficits in planning and initiating goal-oriented behaviors,
✓ lack of motivation,
✓ limited ability to initiate activities,
✓ impulsive behaviors, and
✓ faulty awareness and denial of deficit areas.

We are all constantly bombarded by new information. In our fast-paced society, it's often difficult to keep up with the many demands in our lives. People who experience these cognitive challenges may encounter the following problems:

✓ trouble following through with planned activities;

✓ loss of important items;

✓ illegible documents;

✓ failure to return phone calls;

✓ missed appointments and lack of adherence to prior commitments;

✓ inability to prioritize daily activities; and

✓ disorganization at home, school, or work.

Detailed information on the causes of memory and cognitive deficits and potential medically based treatments is beyond the scope of this book. However, the following websites provide helpful information on how memory and cognition work, types of memory and attention, diagnoses and symptoms, treatment, prevention and screening, alternative therapy, specific conditions, related issues, clinical trials, and research:

✓ **Children and Adults with Attention Deficit/Hyperactivity Disorders (CHADD)**: http://www.chadd.org

✓ **National Institute on Aging**: http://www.nia.nih.gov

✓ **National Institutes of Health**: http://www.nih.gov

✓ **National Institute of Mental Health**: http://www.nimh.nih.gov

✓ **National Institute of Neurological Disorders and Stroke**: http://www.ninds.nih.gov

TREATMENT APPROACHES

As with communication issues, it is important to first differentially diagnose the aspects of cognition to sort out relative strengths and weaknesses. One should limit factors that may adversely influence a person's abilities from one day to the next. Causes may include sleep problems, depression, stress, heat, and external distractions. For many individuals, a neuropsychological evaluation is helpful in which memory, problem solving, visual-spatial skills, language skills, and executive functioning skills are tested. The tests are comprehensive and will more clearly describe cognitive skills—both weak and strong.

Cognitive rehabilitation has two parts: restoring the actual cognitive skill and teaching strategies to compensate for the impaired ability. The use of state-of-the-art technology as well as strategies that do not involve technology are often needed.

RESTORATIVE APPROACH

The first part of cognitive retraining—restoring skills—typically includes exercises to improve attention, concentration, memory, organization, perception, judgment, and problem-solving skills. Treatment most often uses a drill-and-practice method with increasingly challenging tasks. Cognitive abilities are expected to improve, much like a muscle gets stronger with increased exercise. Stimuli gradually increase in difficulty.

A criticism of this method is that the cognitive retraining exercises are essentially artificial and have little relevance to real-world functional cognitive challenges. However, quite a bit of research supports the notion that appropriate practice techniques can help improve memory, learning, and cognition. The premise is that new neurological pathways are formed and improved performance enhances cognitive abilities when clients are confronted with real-world challenges.

COMPENSATORY APPROACH

The second component of cognitive retraining is learning to use strategies, compensatory techniques, and tools to cope with weaker areas. Learning to use these tools not only compensates for impaired ability, but also may help rebuild the skill itself. The compensatory approach to improving memory and cognition generally focuses on the functional activities of daily living.

Assistive technology tools can help a person plan, organize, and keep track of responsibility. There are a wide variety of tools that can help people be more independent and successful with memory and cognitively challenging tasks. Calendars, schedules, task lists, contact information, timers, alarms, the Livescribe Pulse Pen, the iPod touch, cell phones, online resources, and computers can help clients manage, store, and retrieve information as well as improve time management, memory, and new learning. Prior to turning to technology-based solutions, it may be helpful to work on tasks such as:

✓ establishing routines;
✓ organizing and reducing clutter;
✓ minimizing distractions and stress;
✓ establishing a supportive environment;
✓ engaging in cognitively challenging activities;
✓ breaking down seemingly overwhelming tasks into manageable pieces in order of priority and doing them one at a time;
✓ using calendars to improve organization, memory, and communication; and

✓ using timers and alarms to help users remember to take medication, leave for appointments, or track time during a task.

CALENDARS, TIME MANAGEMENT, TO-DO LISTS, NOTES, SCHEDULES, AND TIMERS

There are many technologies available to help individuals become more organized and efficient. There is no one correct time management or organizational system. However, if not properly set up, too many systems can make things more difficult. It is important that each system provides a way for people to easily refer to their contacts, calendar, to-do lists, and notes—whether it is paper based or electronic. Easy access with a backup is critical. Digital systems can be backed up on a computer or hard drive. Paper-based systems need to have a phone number to call and "reward if found" information in a visible spot in case of loss. Users want to avoid clutter and lots of little notes and reminders scattered in different places. It's important to keep home and school or home and work lives in one place and to keep your system with you wherever you go for quick reference as needed. It is often helpful to have both an electronic and paper system in place. Mobile devices are great for quickly accessing phone numbers, calendar information, and reminder systems. Paper systems may be easier for note-taking while on the phone or at a meeting.

There are a multitude of online calendars, Apple and Droid apps, and other products that can help manage time and schedules. Below is a sampling of available resources. Please be sure to search online for the newest products available. More products become available on almost a daily basis!

Awesome Note (+ ToDo)
by BRIDworks
http://www.bridworks.com
- Apple app
- This is a to-do manager and note-taking application.
- A variety of views can be used to manage the needs of students, parents, and professionals.
- Each folder is color coded and has a calendar so that tasks can be efficiently managed and ideas and notes can be recorded during the day.
- Tasks can be assigned due dates and listed in a checklist.

- Pictures and maps can be attached to notes and appointments.
- The app features full sync capabilities with Google Docs and Evernote so it can be used on a desktop or laptop computer.
- All data can be backed up online.
- $3.99

2Do Tasks Done in Style

by Guided Ways Technologies, Ltd

http://www.2doapp.com/en/2Do/features.html

- Apple app
- This is a multifeatured, clear, and easy-to-use to-do list.
- It features color coding, tags, tabbed entries, checklists, alarms, and password protection.
- It has multidevice sync with iCal and Outlook.
- Calendars can be shared using MobileMe.
- Includes location aware tasks.
- $6.99

30 Boxes

http://30boxes.com

- This is a web-based calendar solution with a to-do list where you can add, edit, and remove tasks as well as tag them for organization.
- This site now integrates with many other online social services.
- An Apple app is available.
- Free

Evernote

http://www.evernote.com

- Evernote.com is a free service where you can upload/keep notes, photos, web page clips, lists, and more.
- Users can upload 500MB per month for a free account.
- Photos and notes are searchable using tags, which are multiple key words that can be used to search for an item.
- This app can be used on the web, on a Windows or Mac computer, and also on mobile devices including the Apple iPhone and Droid phone.
- Free

Google Calendar
by Google
http://calendar.google.com

- This is a free time management application.
- The interface is similar to desktop calendar applications such as Microsoft Outlook and iCal and their calendar files can be imported.
- It supports view modes such as weekly, monthly, and agenda.
- Information is stored online, not on the computer, so it is accessible from any computer.
- Multiple calendars can be added and shared, allowing various levels of permissions for the users. This enables collaboration and sharing of schedules between groups.
- General online calendars can often be integrated into the calendar.
- It can be synchronized with mobile devices, PC applications (Microsoft Outlook) via third party software, and natively with Apple's iCal.
- If users are using Gmail, certain words that indicate a meeting or appointment may trigger an "add to calendar" button.
- Google offers a mini-calendar widget that allows users to view their agenda without going online. It can be placed on the desktop or docked on the sidebar.
- The calendar can be synced with many phones such as the BlackBerry and iPhone.
- There is now a Google Calendar Apple app for $6.99.
- Free

iCal
by Apple
http://www.apple.com

- Users can create multiple calendars (e.g., a child has one for school and one for sports practices) and view them in a single window or individually.
- iCal allows users to produce e-mail invitations using contact information from their Address Book, update their guest list, and keep track of responses.
- Users can search for information using Spotlight.
- Virtual sticky notes can be added and shared or synced with others.
- The calendar can be synced to an iPhone or other mobile phone, PDA, iPad, or iPod touch. With a MobileMe account, contacts and calendars stay up to date wirelessly across multiple Mac computers, iPhones, iPod touches, iPads, and the web.
- This application is included with Mac OS X.

iStudiez Pro

by Andriy Kachalo and Michael Balashoff

http://www.istudiez.com

- Apple app
- This is a comprehensive student organizer to help plan for schedules, homework, grades, and projects.
- It offers a multifunctional interactive calendar to help track and manage events and assignments.
- Reminders can be set up and data can be backed up.
- It is available in many languages.
- $2.99

iPrompts

by HandHold Adaptive

http://www.handholdadaptive.com

- Apple app
- This visual prompting application can be used with the iPad, iPod touch, and iPhone.
- It is helpful for children and individuals with communication and cognitive challenges.
- It includes several easy-to-use, visual prompting templates (no audio prompts or voice output) to help individuals transition from one activity to the next, understand upcoming events, make choices, and focus on the task at hand.
- Captions can be edited for each image, allowing users to create social stories.
- A visual countdown timer displays an image of the caregiver's choice, along with a graphical countdown timer (set to any duration).
- Users can create visual prompts to adapt to sudden changes or situations.
- Hundreds of stock images are included within iPrompts and images can be added.
- $49.99

Jott

by Nuance Communications

http://jott.com

- Jott enables users to make a phone call (866-JOTT-123) and turns spoken utterances into text.
- Users can dictate text messages for e-mail or web updates.

- The voice-to-text transcription can be used to help with memory and organization by sending texts and e-mails as reminders for appointments or tasks.
- Jott offers several different applications for desktop computers, Microsoft Outlook, iPhones, and BlackBerry devices.
- Monthly rates vary depending on usage.

Microsoft Outlook 2010

by Microsoft Corporation

http://www.office.microsoft.com/en-us/outlook

- Outlook is a personal information manager. It is available alone or as part of Microsoft Office.
- It can be used to manage e-mail, tasks, a calendar, contacts, notes, journaling, and web browsing.
- It can be integrated with devices such as BlackBerry phones or other smartphones with Office Mobile.
- Multiple calendars can be created and viewed alone or together and shared online.
- Outlook 2010 contains all of the features of Outlook 2007, plus grouping of conversations and a ribbon interface that is more accessible.
- Windows and Mac
- $149.99 (with the Home and Student bundle) or $279.99 (with the Home and Business bundle)

NoteMaster

by Kabuki Vision

http://www.kabukivision.com

- Apple app
- Users can create notes with text, bulleted lists, images, and headers so that they can be organized.
- The app syncs with Google Docs.
- $3.99

Picture Planner

by Cognitopia Software

http://www.cognitopia.com

- Picture Planner is a picture-based personal organizer. It works well as a calendar for individuals who are unable to read or have cognitive challenges.

- Users can create customized, picture-based daily schedules for school, self-care, or chores. Users can upload their own pictures or use photos that are included.
- The schedule uses pictures, text, and text-to-speech and can be printed or exported to other devices.
- Recurring activities, pop-up reminders, and a simple user interface make it easy to use for individuals who are unable to use calendars such as Microsoft Outlook or Google Calendar.
- $199.00

Pocket PicturePlanner
by Cognitopia
http://www.cognitopia.com/iphone.html
- Apple app
- This app needs to be used with Picture Planner described above, which is customizable on a desktop computer.
- Users can view, track, and get reminders for activities and events on the calendar.
- All pictures have text and text-to-speech.
- There are activities for scheduled events, which are organized into categories such as: What are you doing? With who? When? Where? What should you wear? What should you bring?
- Pocket PicturePlanner needs to be synchronized to a licensed copy of Picture Planner 3.0 to enter new information.
- Free

Remember the Milk
http://www.rememberthemilk.com
- This is a web-based task management solution. It allows the user to organize tasks into tabs and tags, and make time-specific tasks with automatic reminders and repeat intervals. It also has collaborative features.
- Users can receive reminders via e-mail, SMS, Google Talk, Skype, and instant messenger.
- Multiple lists with notes can be created and the task cloud displays what needs to be done.
- The map shows where tasks are located in the real world and plans the best way to get things done.
- Free or $25 a year for the pro version

rminder

http://www.rminder.com

- This program sends voice and text reminders to a designated phone. The user or another person programs reminders with specific text, and then on the specified time and date, the recipient receives the message via voice and/or text.
- There is a free option that has a limit of eight reminders a month (two per week).

Ta-da Lists

by 37 Signals

http://www.tadalist.com

- This is a free website to generate to-do lists.
- It is web-based so it can be accessed online from any computer and shared with others.
- The My Lists page shows all of the lists a user has created with the number of items remaining listed.
- The dot in front of the to-do list indicates how much is left to do on a list—the bigger the dot, the more items left to complete.
- Windows, Mac, and iPhone/iPad
- Free

TextMinder SMS

by Adam Alexander

http://txtminder.net

- Apple app
- This app enables users to have text messages sent to their phones at designated times as often as they want.
- $1.99

Time Timer

http://www.timetimer.com

- Apple app
- This app helps users judge how much time is left.
- A high contrast, large dial of numbers shows in red the amount of time left for a task.
- As time passes, the red disk gets smaller.
- You can customize it to any time (including hours, minutes, and seconds).
- $4.99

TrackClass
http://www.trackclass.com
- Free web-based program to help students stay up to date with assignments, take notes, remember events, and stay organized.
- Reminders can be sent out by e-mail or text message.
- Notes can be written within the application.
- iCal export is supported.
- Files can be uploaded and tracked.
- The program can be synced to mobile devices.
- Free

VoCal Voice Reminders!
by GZero Ltd
http://www.gzero.com
- Apple app
- Users record a reminder with their voice, set a time and date for the reminder to alert them, and then save and close the app.
- No written input is needed.
- Unlimited reminders are included in the price.
- $3.99

STUDY SKILLS TOOLS

Technology tools can greatly enhance an individual's ability to learn new information. Often a combination of traditional studying approaches combined with innovative cutting-edge resources creates a more motivating environment for the learner. Online flashcards; software that provides assistance with reading, writing, and organization; and a pen that can record audio, when used creatively, can empower learners to become more successful. These tools allow individuals learning new information—whether they are students or professionals—greater independence in learning by customizing software to take advantage of learning strengths and to help compensate for learning weaknesses. Many of these products are also highlighted in other sections of this book.

FLASHCARD PROGRAMS
There are a variety of web-based programs that allow users to create and use flashcards for online study or studying with the iPad or other portable app device or phone. Most require the user to set up an account. Many can either be private or shared with others. Students can pool their

resources and share flashcards created for studying or therapists can create them for clients. It is usually possible to import pictures and/or audio and many use "tags," which are keywords to group the content in different ways. Multiple languages are supported in quite a few of them and most offer a system to help study missed items.

Cue Card 1.51
by Wade Brainerd
http://www.download.com/3000-2051-10075304.html
- Users decide what to work on and CueCard will quiz the user.
- CueCard features smart testing, which automatically focuses on the items that are the most difficult.
- It offers printing (including custom page layouts and sizes), pictures and sounds on cards, Unicode support, card formatting, a multilingual user interface, and more.
- Windows
- Free

Flashcard Touch
by Agilis Lab
http://www.agilislab.com
- Apple app
- This app can access the millions of premade flashcards from the Quizlet community (which has more than 800,000 registered users).
- Flashcards can be easily shared with others.
- Flashcards can be created using a built-in online definition feature or created in Quizlet, then downloaded to the device.
- $4.99

FlashcardExchange
by Tuolumne Technology Group
http://www.flashcardexchange.com
- Users can create their own online flashcards, use the flashcards already online, and share them online for free.
- To find flashcards that were already created by others, users can go to the flashcard directory and search through headings such as Early Education, Elementary School, and High School. Early Education includes headings such as Dolch and Word Walls. Users then can edit the previously created lists and then add them to their own sets of flashcards.

- They are available in many languages.
- An additional charge is required to add images, download the flash-cards, or add a third side to the card.
- Users can track performance and play a memory game with the cards.
- $4.99 with the Mental Case app

Quizlet
http://quizlet.com
- This site contains interactive online flashcards.
- Users can access millions of flashcards created by other students and teachers, or create their own and share them.
- Quizlet takes information in "sets" rather than a single flashcard, then pairs the answer and question together. This sets up games the user can employ for studying.
- Quizlet offers several options for studying:
  - o Familiarize shows flashcards with additional options to show the question and answer at the same time or to quiz in reverse.
  - o The Learn button quizzes users on the material one question at a time.
  - o The Test option uses multiple-choice, true/false, or write-in formats.

- Images can be uploaded to the flashcards.
- Free

StudyStack
by John Weidner
http://www.studystack.com
- This is a free, online program that can be used to access already included study stacks or make customized stacks.
- A stack of "virtual cards" contains information about a certain subject.
- Users review the information, discarding the cards that were already learned and keeping the others for additional review.
- Each card can show multiple pieces of information, and the whole stack can be automatically sorted by any one of the pieces of information.
- The data for a study stack can be displayed as flashcards, a matching game, a word search puzzle, and a hangman game.
- The information can be exported to other devices.
- Free

SOCIAL BOOKMARKING AND ANNOTATION

The Internet is playing an increasingly important role in the way we obtain and organize new information. It used to be that people would print web pages onto paper and highlight and file them or type the URLs for future reference. There are now many tools that are extremely helpful with online information management. Internet users can share, organize, and search for information using social bookmarking tools. Users save links to web pages and can make them public or private, or specify e-mail addresses that can view them. The system can rank a resource based on the number of viewers who have bookmarked the site using different "tags."

Diigo
http://www.diigo.com
- Diigo is a free social bookmarking website that allows users to bookmark, tag, and highlight web pages.
- Users can add "sticky notes" and highlight any part of a page. All of the markings can be extracted to collect for later use.
- Information can be private or shared with others.
- Users can also search for items and do group-based collaborative research on this social bookmarking site.
- Diigo can be used with many browsers and offers Apple apps and Android apps.
- Diigo can be very effectively used from multiple computers and portable devices:
  - o when writing reports;
  - o to organize websites, pictures, notes, bookmarks, screenshots, audio, and documents; and
  - o to assist with memory and communication.

- Free

SOFTWARE WITH EMBEDDED STUDY TOOLS

Quite a few of the assistive technology tools that were reviewed earlier in this book to help with reading and writing are very helpful for learning new information. Products with text-to-speech capabilities can improve new learning due to the increased retention of written information when it is simultaneously read aloud and highlighted by a computer. Brainstorming software and other tools to help users learn new information presented graphically can be quite effective. The ability to mark up printed info when studying is also very helpful.

Almost all word processing programs offer the ability to highlight text. Some also enable the user to extract the highlighted material into a separate file for studying. Easy access to bookmarking, note-taking, summarizing, paraphrasing, and a dictionary are helpful study skill features of some word processors. Text notes are helpful for visual processors, aiding the user to revisit and study important material. Using voice notes, users can dictate information such as oral summarizing and paraphrasing.

Below are some products that can be used to improve study skills. Most have been described in previous chapters.

- ✓ **E-Text Reader 3.0**: http://www.readingmadeez.com/products/EtextReader.html
- ✓ **iAnnotate for iPad**: http://www.ajidev.com/iannotate
- ✓ **Inspiration 9**: http://www.inspiration.com
- ✓ **Kurzweil 3000**: http://www.kurzweiledu.com
- ✓ **Livescribe Echo Pen**: http://www.livescribe.com
- ✓ **Microsoft Word 2007**: http://www.microsoft.com
- ✓ **Read&Write Gold**: http://www.texthelp.com
- ✓ **Read:OutLoud 6**: http://www.donjohnston.com
- ✓ **RecallPlus Study Software**: http://www.recallplus.com
- ✓ **WYNN Literacy Software**: http://www.freedomscientific.com

ONLINE COLLABORATION

There are now many technology tools that allow individuals who are far apart to collaborate online, which can be very effective when studying or completing a group project.

- ✓ **Screen sharing or desktop sharing** can be used so that an individual enables another person to view his or her desktop or screen from a distance and view videos, software, or documents. In some cases, the person can hand over the ability to control the desktop to the person viewing from a distance.
- ✓ **Voice Over Internet Protocol** (VOIP) is the ability to talk over the Internet.
- ✓ **Online collaborative workspaces** allow groups of people to work together on common documents in various formats either synchronously (at the same time) or asynchronously (at different times). This includes the following:
  - ▶ **Google Docs**: http://www.docs.google.com
  - ▶ **PiratePad**: http://www.piratepad.net
  - ▶ **Sync.in**: http://sync.in
  - ▶ **TitanPad**: http://www.titanpad.com

✓ **Videoconferencing/video chat** allows two or more locations to interact via two-way video and audio transmissions simultaneously. People can see each other while speaking.

Skype
http://www.skype.com
- Voice and video calls can be made to anyone else on Skype for free.
- Conference calls with three or more people are available.
- Instant messaging, file transfer, and screen sharing are available.
- Free

ooVoo
http://www.oovoo.com
- This site features two-way video chats.
- Users can use text chat and send files.
- Free

INTERACTIVE COMPUTER SOFTWARE TO IMPROVE MEMORY AND COGNITION

There are many software programs on the market to improve cognitive functioning. They are helpful for children who experience attention and learning difficulties as well as people with documented impairments due to head injury, brain surgery, or stroke. Programs geared toward keeping the brain "fit" during the natural aging process are also becoming increasingly popular.

Brain Fitness Program
by Posit Science
http://www.positscience.com
- This program was designed to sharpen the brain's auditory system using a series of carefully controlled listening tasks in order to improve the brain's ability to receive, interpret, and store auditory information.
- The goal of the Brain Fitness Program is to improve overall thinking, focus, and memory.
- Multiple exercises are provided that target different cognitive functions such as sound processing when presented quickly, distinguish-

ing between similar sounds, remembering the order of sounds, and improving working and short-term memory.

- The program gets harder and easier automatically in response to the user's performance.
- Data are collected to document progress.
- Users are encouraged to practice daily.
- Windows and Mac
- $395.00

BrainBuilder
by Advanced Brain Technologies
http://www.brainbuilder.com

- The exercises are organized into three groups—auditory, visual, and focus. The goal is to improve visualization, conceptualization, and sequential processing.
- The program automatically adjusts the level of difficulty and tracks performance.
- Users select 15- or 30-minute sessions and easy, moderate, or challenging tasks.
- Each session starts and finishes with a relaxing video clip to calm the brain and classical music accompanies the training sessions.
- A brain diary is included so that users can become more aware of lifestyle factors that may influence cognitive functioning.
- An online connection is not required and the program can accommodate up to five users.
- Windows
- $249.95

Building Thinking Skills Software
by The Critical Thinking Co.
http://www.criticalthinking.com

- This program provides verbal and nonverbal reasoning activities to improve vocabulary, reading, writing, math, logic, and figural-spatial skills in children, as well as visual and auditory processing.
- Exercises involve describing characteristics; distinguishing similarities and differences; and identifying and completing sequences, classifications, and analogies.
- The activities are sequenced and in a game format.
- Each skill is presented first in the concrete figural-spatial form and then in the abstract verbal form.
- Windows and Mac
- $36.99

Captain's Log

by Brain Train

http://www.braintrain.com

- Game-like brain-building software is used to build attention, reasoning, listening skills, memory, self-esteem, hand-eye coordination, impulse control, and quick processing speed in users of all ages and every ability level.
- Five programs focus on working memory and auditory attention.
- Programs use mazes, block designs, puzzles, visual codes and sequences, and simple to complex shapes to address visual-spatial deficits.
- This software uses sequences of numbers, letters, and words of varying complexity to work on visual and verbal memory deficits.
- Time limits on many programs encourage users to work efficiently and rapidly.
- Windows
- $1,995.00

Mind Benders Software

by The Critical Thinking Co.

http://www.criticalthinking.com

- This software offers several different levels of deductive thinking puzzles.
- Users develop the logic, reading comprehension, and mental organization skills in order to solve the puzzles and analyze each Mind Benders story and its clues, identifying logical associations between people, places, and things.
- This software is produced for middle school students.
- Windows and Mac
- $25.99

Revenge of the Logic Spiders

by The Critical Thinking Co.

http://www.criticalthinking.com

- Each activity was produced to sharpen reasoning and comprehension through multiple-choice word problems that increase in difficulty. Only the correct inferences and deductions allow students to escape the hungry spiders.
- There are 116 logic problems and three maze sizes.
- Targeted for grades 6–12.
- Windows and Mac
- $19.99

Thinkin' Things: Collection 1, 2 and 3
by Edmark
http://www.childrenssoftwareonline.com
- This software was developed for ages 3–7 and improves visual and auditory memory, while building logical, musical, spatial, and kinesthetic thinking skills.
- It provides opportunities to compare and contrast attributes.
- The software enhances children's observation and perception abilities.
- It introduces hypotheses, testing of rules, and the relationship between scientific exploration and creativity.
- Windows and Mac
- $14.98

ONLINE PROGRAMS TO IMPROVE MEMORY AND COGNITION

BrainFlex
by BrainReady
http://www.brainready.com/brainflex
- This site includes online brain games to train the brain and allow people of all ages to get a daily brain workout.
- No registration is required.
- Adobe Flash Player is required and a download is available at the site.
- Free

BrainSpark
by Scientific Learning
http://www.brainsparklearning.com
- This site includes several interactive online learning programs designed to maximize a child's learning potential by building cognitive skills such as sequencing, processing rate, attention, recall and memory, and knowledge.
- It is designed to be used 30 minutes a day, 5 days a week.
- It provides a weekly progress report.
- Learners who need more comprehensive brain training have access to BrainPro tutors.
- Contact providers on website for pricing

Challenging Our Minds

by Cognitive Enhancement Systems

http://www.challenging-our-minds.com

- Challenging Our Minds (COM) is a cognitive enhancement system designed by a neuropsychologist to develop and enhance cognitive functions across the domains of attention, executive skills, memory, visuospatial skills, problem-solving skills, communication, and psychosocial skills.
- It is a subscription website providing games for all children ranging from gifted to those with learning disabilities, attention problems, processing problems, and developmental disabilities.
- The system automatically keeps track of where users stop working during a session and will start back on the next session at the same point. It is suggested that the user interact with the system 30–60 minutes a day.
- Windows and Mac
- $25.00 a month for 3-month individual subscription

Lumosity

by Lumos Labs

http://www.lumosity.com

- The program consists of a number of different brain training games that are designed to target and improve certain cognitive thinking applications, such as memory, speed, flexibility, and attention.
- Games increase in difficulty as users improve.
- The overall format of the program is easy to use and navigate.
- Each game has a visual instruction area that shows how the games are played.
- There are Apple apps for some of the games.
- Free

MyBrainTrainer

by MyBrainTrainer LLC

http://www.mybraintrainer.com

- MyBrainTrainer.com contains short, individual exercises designed to stimulate different parts of the brain with intense mental focus.
- The premise is that regular mental workouts of 10–20 minutes daily can improve cognitive function and brain processing speed.
- The Basic Training program is 21 days. Its goal is to improve the speed of information processing and the ability to focus.
- The exercises provide immediate feedback with respect to performance (e.g., speed, accuracy, consistency, perceptual threshold),

so that progress can be monitored. As brain processing speed increases, the exercises automatically become more challenging.
- Windows and Mac
- $9.95 for 3 months or $29.95 for a year

Parrot Software
by Parrot Software
http://www.parrotsoftware.com
- There are many lessons presented in a multiple-choice format with customizable levels that work on different aspects of cognition such as: memory for directions, hierarchical attention training, memory for animated sequences, visual memory, word memory and discrimination, word recognition, auditory and visual instructions, multitasking, visual motor memory, logical thinking, inferential reading comprehension, and time management.
- Windows and Mac
- $24.95 monthly subscription for a single user

APPS TO IMPROVE MEMORY AND COGNITION

Apps to improve memory and cognition are being added every day to the various app stores for mobile devices. Here are just a few to try.

BrainPOP Featured Movie
by BrainPOP
http://www.brainpop.com/apps/about
- Apple app
- School-age children can watch a new movie each day. The videos are short, entertaining, captioned, and informative.
- Knowledge is tested with an interactive quiz.
- Free

Jigsaw Puzzles
by Intuitive Innovations
http://www.intuitiveinnovationssoftware.com
- Apple app
- Users select the level of difficulty, as well as the picture for the puzzle.
- Fingers are used to slide the pieces into place.

- Simple puzzles can be used to teach cause and effect and work on cognitive skills such as attention and focus.
- $1.99

Lumosity Games
by Lumosity
http://www.lumosity.com/mobile

- Apple app
- Lumosity offers a number of apps including:
  o Chalkboard Challenge: Works on comparing values, accurate estimations, and mental computation.
  o Color Match: Works on avoiding errors, resisting temptation, and impulse control.
  o Memory Matrix: Works on visual recall.
  o Speed Brain: Works on thinking faster, quicker reaction times, and speeding up cognitive processes.

- Games are free or $0.99

Match 10
by Sawmill Code, LLC
http://www.sawmillcode.com

- Apple app
- This is the classic game of concentration with multiple levels.
- Players can upload their own pictures to use.
- In addition to working on improving attention and memory, parents and therapists can work on verbal expression and social skills while playing the game.
- $0.99

MeMoves
by ThinkingMoves
http://www.thinkingmoves.com

- Apple app
- This app was developed to help calm, focus, and align children with autism and related disorders with the help of music and movement.
- Users perform finger puzzles to the beat of music and watch as the screen responds.
- There are multiple sensitivity settings, calming graphics and music, and more than 30 puzzles.
- $2.99

Seek and Find
by Gnosis Game
http://gnosisgames.com/seekandfind

- Apple app
- The app includes games to improve attention, focus, and speed of processing.
- It has 45 levels with increasing complexity and challenge.
- $2.99

CAUSE AND EFFECT RESOURCES

Don Johnston
http://DonJohnston.com

- This site offers a variety of software such as Press-to-Play, Cause and Effect Cinema, and Attention Getter/Attention Teens.
- $30.00–$80.00 for various software programs

HelpKidzLearn
http://Helpkidzlearn.com

- This is a collection of software for young children and those with learning difficulties to play online.
- It can be played just using the space bar or a few other keys, and it can be used with special switches.
- The software is split into four sections: Games and Quizzes, Stories and Songs, Creative Play, and Find Out About.
- Free

Hiyah.net
http://hiyah.net

- This software has a full variety of switch activities for learners with multiple or significant special needs.
- The activities listed were developed because they can be used with switches, are simple, and don't require downloads.
- Free

Judy Lynn Software
http://judylynn.com

- A number of high-quality programs are available.
- Intro to Cause & Effect—$39.00
- Animated Toys II—$49.00

Northern Grid
http://www.northerngrid.org

- SENSwitcher consists of programs designed to help people with profound and multiple learning difficulties, those who need to develop skills with assistive input devices, and very young children new to computers.
- The program can be run directly from the website or downloaded for use on stand-alone PC or Macintosh computers.
- It includes 132 high-quality animated activities that can be operated by a wide range of input devices.
- Free

Shiny Learning
http://www.shinylearning.co.uk

- The products on this site can be accessed using a variety of input devices such as switches or keyboard as well as the mouse.
- Many programs can be edited, allowing you to create your own tailored activities.
- There are free games online and software available for purchase.

ADDITIONAL DEVICES TO ASSIST WITH MEMORY AND COGNITION

A number of tools and devices are available to help with memory, organization, time management, and executive functioning skills.

Voice Memos on iPod touch, iPhone, and iPad

- Users can record any audio using the Apple earphones with remote and microphone or an external microphone. It will record while users are searching online or reading e-mail.
- Organize the memos by selecting labels or creating your own.
- Recordings can be synced back to an iTunes account and shared.

Loc8tor Lite
by Loc8tor, Ltd.
http://www.loc8tor.com

- Loc8tor Lite helps find important possessions with the use of a homing device.

- In the Locate mode, audio beeps and the on-screen directional display guide users to mislaid tagged items.
- In the Alert mode, an invisible safety zone can be established around the Loc8tor Lite, alerting the user with audio-visual and vibration alarms should tagged items move out of the set boundary.
- Small, discrete tags and a compact handheld unit direct users from up to 600 feet to within 1 inch of the mislaid item.
- $79.99

WatchMinder2

http://www.watchminder.com

- This is a programmable vibrating reminder watch that looks like a standard sports wristwatch but the watch vibrates and a reminder message discreetly appears.
- The watch can be used as a memory and cueing device for individuals with memory dysfunction. It comes with 60 preprogrammed messages.
- Personalized messages can also be entered into the memory of the watch. The watch has 30 daily alarms. A person's entire day can be preprogrammed, with alarms activated at specific times of the day and messages/reminders displayed.
- Children can use the watch to self-monitor their own behavior.
- Older students find the watch helpful for time management and pacing during exams.
- $69.00

CHAPTER 11

GAMES AND FREE, ONLINE, INTERACTIVE ACTIVITIES

Many people believe that playing games is a waste of time. This could not be further from the truth. Traditional and computer-based games are often gold mines in terms of helping people to improve their reading, writing, speaking, understanding, and cognitive skills. It is often hard to distinguish between interactive multimedia sites designed for therapy and education and games for leisure and recreation. Board games, card games, strategy games, word games, and even games of luck, when used appropriately, offer enormous benefits. Children may be more easily engaged in activities and practice new skills without realizing that there is an educational process taking place. Adults can reduce stress, enjoy acquiring new skills, and find new ways to interact with others.

Brain research shows that brain pathways improve with practice. It's helpful if we can find ways for people with communication and cognitive challenges to practice the skills they are working on with enjoyable activities. Games can be effective tools for people with both severe and subtle deficits. Rules and activities often need to be modified to make them appropriate for each person. This can be accomplished by exploring and selecting options that are provided with the gamer by varying the amount of assistance provided during the game.

As with other types of assistive technology, keep in mind the person's goals, visual impairments, fine motor abilities, cognitive and communication strengths and weaknesses, and interests.

RESOURCES FOR ADAPTED GAMES

Some people may benefit from products that were created to make games easier to play for people with disabilities. Products may be made larger and easier to manipulate. There are also games that were produced to be used to improve communication and cognition. Please refer to the following listings for more information:

- ✓ **Nanogames**: http://www.arcess.com (30 fun, adapted games)
- ✓ **RJ Cooper & Associates**: http://www.rjcooper.com (game controllers)
- ✓ **AudioGames.net**: http://www.audiogames.net (games for the visually impaired)

NEW EDUCATIONAL GAMING TECHNOLOGIES

Cell phones, iPods, iPads, Playstations, Wiis, Nintendo DSIs, computers, and other devices for playing games have become commonplace—for both children and adults. A few of them lend themselves particularly well to helping people who have communication and cognitive challenges.

There are helpful games that come already installed on many computers. They can be used to improve attention, concentration, thinking, and use of the mouse or other selection method.

- ✓ For PCs, go to the Start Menu, then Programs, then Games.
- ✓ For Macs, go to http://www.apple.com/downloads/macosx/games.

These sites may be helpful when searching for mainstream games:

- ✓ **Amazon.com**: http://www.amazon.com
- ✓ **Best Buy**: http://www.bestbuy.com
- ✓ **Children's Software Online**: http://www.childrenssoftwareonline.com
- ✓ **Board Game Central**: http://boardgamecentral.com
- ✓ **Knowledge Adventure**: http://www.knowledgeadventure.com
- ✓ **Smart Kids Software**: http://www.smartkidssoftware.com
- ✓ **GameStop**: http://www.gamestop.com

Spider solitaire (the easiest level) and solitaire (made easier by turning over one card at a time and showing the outline dragging options) are very helpful when helping individuals become more adept at using the mouse, to improve visual-perceptual skills, and to practice verbal skills.

FREE INTERACTIVE WEBSITES

The following free online resources for computers do not require membership or fees. Some require logins and passwords. They may require Macromedia Shockwave or a Java platform—both of which can be downloaded at no charge. Depending on the Internet connection speed, most downloads are fast. Some games are played alone, while others engage the play of others who are online. Clinicians can adapt them all to work toward therapy goals. Spend a bit of time checking out the sites to determine which are best and how they should be used. They can provide hundreds of hours of practice working on communication and cognition.

Below is a brief description of sites that are helpful for people with communication and cognitive challenges.

AARP Games
http://www.aarp.org/games
- AARP's site features online puzzles, jigsaws, and other interactive games.
- There are clear instructions with minimal advertising interruptions.
- Free

All inPlay: Games With Vision
http://www.allinplay.com
- A few multiplayer games are fully accessible and were designed to work with a screen reader or screen magnifier.
- The player can practice against the computer or play against others.
- There is a free trial period, and then access to popular card games cost less than $8.00 a month.

Autism Games
http://sites.google.com/site/autismgames
- This is a website with a collection of games with strong social components designed to be used with children with autism.
- There are tips and strategies for making games and play more educational and more fun.
- The games are listed with print and video instructions and three levels of difficulty. A separate list of learning objectives is available as well.

Bry-Back Manor

http://www.bry-backmanor.org

- This site contains a vast collection of games for download on a Mac and materials to use with children who have special needs.

CBeebies

http://www.bbc.co.uk/cbeebies

- CBeebies online has many preschool characters and lots of fun games, stories, and activities.
- The activities develop computer skills and hand-eye coordination.

Children's Storybooks Online

http://www.magickeys.com/books

- Free online talking eBooks are provided with pictures categorized for young children, older children, and young adults.
- Online jigsaw puzzles, riddles, and games are included.

Discovery Education Brain Boosters

http://school.discoveryeducation.com/brainboosters

- This site offers a categorized archive of challenging Brain Boosters.
- It has activities to improve categorizations, lateral thinking, logic, number and math play, reasoning, spatial awareness, and word and letter play.

Funbrain

http://www.funbrain.com

- This site has math, spelling, and creative writing games.
- Each section allows users to start the game over, to switch levels, or to return to the home page to select another game.

Gamequarium

http://www.gamequarium.com

- This site offers more than 1,500 links to online games that are categorized by core content.
- Kids can practice skills with scores and times to record on learning logs.
- Language arts activities include word fun, vocabulary games, parts of speech, sentence structure, spelling, and punctuation.

GCFLearnFree.org

http://www.GCFLearnFree.org

- LearnFree.org is an interactive website designed to help teach functional skills through a variety of free online activities.
- There are different categories of learning available including Everyday Life, Math and Money, Computer Training, Online Classes, and Work and Career.
- The site is clean and easy to navigate. Signing up and using the resource is simple.
- Accessibility options are offered, as is a Spanish version.

Hiyah.net

http://www.hiyah.net

- This website offers free software for children who need cause-effect programs.
- The programs are based on high-interest subjects, such as nursery rhymes, holidays, and birthday themes and operate by pressing the spacebar.

JigZone

http://www.jigzone.com

- This is a great site for puzzles with a wide variety of levels.
- You can determine the pictures, number of pieces, and shape of each puzzle.

JuniorsWeb

http://www.juniorsweb.com

- This site offers games to work toward speech therapy goals of speech, language, and literacy.

LearningPlanet

http://www.learningplanet.com

- LearningPlanet.com provides a wide variety of fun learning activities, educational games, printable worksheets, and powerful tools.
- Apps from the Apple Store are now available related to this site.
- Educational games are provided for kids from pre-K to sixth grade.
- Users can choose a grade level and get a list of games designed to improve their learning skills and proficiency in many different subjects.

ManyThings.org—Interesting Things for ESL Students
http://www.manythings.org
- This site includes quizzes, word games, word puzzles, proverbs, slang expressions, anagrams, a random-sentence generator, and other computer-assisted, language learning activities.

National Geographic Kids
http://www.kids.nationalgeographic.com
- This site has beautiful graphics, games, puzzles, coloring books, and other interactive activities.

ParentPals.com Special Education Games
http://www.parentpals.com/gossamer/pages/Special_Education_Games/index.html
- Parentpals.com offers a wide variety of educational and therapy games to enhance learning and language skills.
- Games are organized by levels of difficulty.

PBS Kids
http://www.pbskids.org
- This site features many games and learning activities related to PBS children's shows.

PrimaryGames
http://www.primarygames.com
- This site offers interactive online games for elementary-age children.
- It is very colorful, requires a Java-enabled browser, and has commercial banner ads.
- The site covers language arts, math, science, and social studies skills.

ReadWriteThink
http://www.readwritethink.org
- This site was produced by the International Reading Association and the National Council of Teachers of English.
- The are hundreds of activities organized by grade level for parents and professionals with accompanying learning objectives.
- This is an excellent resource for many free online interactive games as well as other activities and projects and podcasts.
- There are also many helpful documents about how to do things such as help a child choose a book, help a child edit and revise his work, how to start a blog, and writing for the real world.

Scholastic

http://www.scholastic.com

- This site offers games and activities for kids; activities, information, and advice for parents; lessons, activities, and tools for teachers; and trends, products, and solutions for administrators.

Sheppard Software

http://www.sheppardsoftware.com

- This site offers hundreds of games to learn about categories such as the U.S., world, animals, language arts, health, science, and math.
- There is a special section featuring top game choices for young children.
- Toward the bottom of the initial screen the programs are sorted for age groups including preschool and kindergarten, elementary and early middle school, middle school and high school, college, and adults.

Smarty Games

http://www.smartygames.com

- This is a group of free games for young children. If a child can move an onscreen pointer by mouse, joystick, touch window, trackball, voice, or head pointer, he or she can play these simple games such as dot-to-dots, puzzles, telling time, coloring pictures, and more.

Starfall

http://www.starfall.com

- This is an elementary-level site for phonetic spelling and early reading skills.
- There are more than 20 free interactive stories with a variety of tasks for the emergent reader.
- It is phonics based and requires the child to be able to click and drag.

TumbleBooks

http://www.tumblebooks.com

- The TumbleBookLibrary includes an online collection of animated talking picture books, reading comprehension quizzes, educational games, and professional resources.

Vocabulary and SpellingCity
http://www.spellingcity.com
- This is a series of free, printable online games using a customizable spelling word list. Individuals can enter 5–10 spelling words, and Vocabulary and SpellingCity can turn this list into a word search, a matching game, HangMouse, a crossword puzzle, and much more.

Vocabulary Building Games
http://www.vocabulary.co.il
- This site offers easy-to-use crosswords, word searches, hangman puzzles, jumbles, and a matching game.
- Each activity has three levels of difficulty and provides a wide variety of topics.

CHAPTER 12

INTERNET COMMUNICATION AND LEARNING TOOLS

The web is full of valuable information. It is changing the way that we find and present information. The use of technologies such as the Internet as a teaching tool in schools is now commonplace. Podcasts, instant messaging, text messages, and social networking sites have become mainstream, but individuals with communication, learning, and cognitive challenges often do not know how to take advantage of these new communication and learning tools. Individuals who struggle with reading, writing, thinking, and speaking can benefit greatly from the access to information and communication the Internet offers, but are often not exposed to it. If speaking is difficult, perhaps they can type or send pictures online to express themselves or communicate with live video to benefit from nonverbal communications. If reading is difficult, perhaps podcasts would be a more appropriate way to gather information so that they can listen rather than read. Social networking sites and Twitter can help people connect with others they may not be able to see in person. Below is a brief description of some technology tools that are currently available with helpful examples of each.

BLOGS (WEBLOGS)
- ✓ A blog is a web page made up of short, frequently updated postings that are arranged chronologically.
- ✓ **2E: Twice-Exceptional Newsletter**: http://2enewsletter.blogspot.com

✓ **Teaching Learners with Multiple Special Needs**: http://teachinglearnerswithmultipleneeds.blogspot.com

✓ **Special Education Law Blog**: http://specialeducationlawblog.blogspot.com

CHAT ROOMS

✓ A chat room is an online site in which people can talk by posting messages to people who are on the same site at the same time.

✓ Sometimes the messages are moderated.

✓ There are different rooms for people who have different interests.

DISCUSSION GROUPS, ELECTRONIC MAILING LISTS, AND BULLETIN BOARDS

✓ Discussion groups or lists allow for ongoing discussions among members. They facilitate interaction among members because they enable members to post questions, comments, suggestions, or answers to a large number of people without everyone being available at the same time.

✓ Some are moderated while others automatically accept all postings.

✓ They are typically fully or partially automated through the use of special mailing list software. Some mailing lists archive their postings and these archives are available on the Internet for browsing.

✓ Some mailing lists are open to anyone who wants to join them, while others require an approval from the list owner in order for someone to join. Some are free; others require a fee.

✓ **Children's Disability Lists of Lists**: http://www.comeunity.com/disability/speclists.html

✓ **Commonwealth Center of Excellence in Stroke, Stroke-L List**: http://www.mc.uky.edu/stroke/Stroke-L.htm

E-LEARNING AND DISTANCE EDUCATION (INTERNET/WEB-BASED TRAINING)

✓ Distance education is designed to be used remotely over the Internet.

✓ **120 Online Special Education Graduate Programs**: http://www.gradschools.com/search-programs/online-programs/special-education

✓ **Elluminate**: http://www.elluminate.com

✓ **TWIST at a Distance for Caregivers**: http://www.innovativespeech.com/therapyoptions.index.html

> ► An experienced speech pathologist (and the author of this book) teaches professionals and families how to use technology to improve communication, cognition, and learning.

E-MAIL

> ✓ Users can type and send written messages over the Internet to another person or group of people by use of e-mail addresses.
> ✓ The recipient of the message can read the message at a convenient time using a computer or handheld communication device.
> ✓ Google's free online e-mail system called Gmail is very popular.

INSTANT MESSAGING

> ✓ Instant messaging is a method of Internet and phone communication that allows two or more people to "chat" by sending messages back and forth immediately.
> ✓ Instant messaging users set up "buddy lists" and see when their family, friends, and associates are online and available to exchange messages.
> ✓ Sending a message opens up a small window where the sender and recipient can both see the messages being sent.

PODCASTS

> ✓ A podcast is like an Internet radio show that you can download and listen to at your convenience or listen to directly from the web.
> ✓ The majority of podcasts are MP3 files, which means that a person can listen to them on any MP3 player or on a computer.
> ✓ You can download one of any number of free software programs to your computer such as iTunes. The software programs can capture particular podcasts.
> ✓ For a feel for what podcasts are like, check out these links:
> > ► **LD Podcast**: http://www.ldpodcast.com
> > ► **Johns Hopkins Medicine Podcasts**: http://www.hopkinsmedicine.org/mediaII/Podcasts.html
> > ► **Disability 411**: http://disability411.jinkle.com

RSS FEEDS

> ✓ RSS feeds help connect web authors and their audience.
> ✓ Authors can choose to notify others automatically of new entries or changes to part of a website or blog by creating a feed.
> ✓ Others may choose to be notified automatically of those new entries or changes by subscribing to feeds.

✓ Choosing to receive notification is called "subscribing" to the feed for that part of that website. Along with notification, the subscriber usually gets some form of direct access to the new or changed material.

✓ New browsers have built-in feed detection, subscription, and management.

✓ An example can be found at CNN.com, which will send out headline news.

SCREEN SHARING OR DESKTOP SHARING, WEBINARS, AND ONLINE MEETINGS

✓ Share your computer screen in real time so that everyone sees what you see—regardless of the application, software, or operating system you are using.

✓ Access any remote computer via Internet just like sitting in front of it.

✓ This is often used during video/web conferences.

✓ Programs differ in the number of people who can participate, whether or not people need to download software to participate, and the ability to record the sessions.

✓ Some programs have the capability to have participants join using smartphones.

✓ Most offer real-time collaboration with whiteboards and annotation tools, mouse and keyboard sharing, and instantly changing presenters.

✓ Free for individual use:

  ► **Mikogo**: http://www.mikogo.com
  ► **Skype**: http://www.skype.com

✓ Paid for business use and more attendees and features:

  ► **GoToMeeting**: http://www.gotomeeting.com
  ► **WebEx**: http://www.webex.com
  ► **Glance**: http://www.glance.net
  ► **WebConference.com**: http://www.webconference.com

SOCIAL NETWORKING SITES

✓ Social networking sites allow people to create profiles about themselves and connect or network with other people's profiles.

✓ Once they have networked with a friend, users can then view the profiles of their friend's friends. As they connect with more and more people, their social network expands.

✓ These networks can then be used for fun, for connecting specific groups, for arranging activities, and for networking.

✓ Some popular social networking sites include MySpace, Facebook, and LinkedIn.

✓ Not as well known are the social networking sites created specifically to serve patients and families facing health challenges or individuals who need more protected sites. Check out:

  ▶ **CaringBridge**: http://www.caringbridge.org

    ▫ A free customized website can be created so that family and friends can be kept abreast of the patient's progress through the patient care journal and photo gallery and can post words of encouragement through the guestbook.

    ▫ This program benefits the patient and family alike by keeping concerned loved ones informed of the patient's condition without the need for multiple phone calls or e-mails. It also creates a mini support group for the patient in which people can encourage and motivate the patient.

    ▫ A free CaringBridge application is available from the Apple App Store for iPhone, iPod touch, and iPad users. This streamlined version of the website makes it easy to visit a personal CaringBridge site as well as leave guestbook messages.

TEXT MESSAGING

✓ Text messaging is a communication mode that allows users to exchange short messages.

✓ The short messages are sent to a smartphone, pager, PDA, or other handheld device.

✓ There is a new written language to minimize keystrokes that has become popular with the rise of instant messaging, chat rooms, and text messaging. Explanations of some of these shortened phrases can be found at http://www.netlingo.com/acronyms.php.

✓ It is especially helpful when talking on the phone is inappropriate or inconvenient and you want to communicate in real time.

✓ Young people often would rather send text messages, post messages on social sites, and send instant messages than call someone on the phone or send an e-mail to communicate.

VIDEO CHAT

✓ A video chat or videoconference is a set of interactive telecommunication technologies that allows two or more locations to interact via two-way video and audio at the same time. For people with communication and cognitive challenges, videoconferencing is a great way to communicate because nonverbal communication can augment verbal messages. It's really helpful to see the person with whom you are communicating. Some programs require downloads, others don't. A webcam is needed to capture video. Without a webcam, users can still speak to each other—they just won't see each other.

Skype
http://www.skype.com
- Users can make free voice and video calls to anyone else on Skype.
- Conference calls with three or more people are available.
- Instant messaging, file transfer, and screen sharing are offered options.
- Free

ooVoo
http://www.oovoo.com
- ooVoo offers two-way video chats.
- Users can also text chat and send files to others.
- Premium accounts are available.
- Free

Google voice and video chat
http://www.google.com/chat/video
- There is a free plug-in to Gmail that needs to be downloaded for this to work.
- Users can record their video chats.
- Free

VIDEO ON THE WEB
- ✓ This technology enables users to view videos over the Internet
- ✓ Streaming media is a technology that delivers audio, video, images, and text to the user without downloading the entire file. It feeds the user only the portion of the file he needs at the moment.
  - ▶ **YouTube.com:** This site offers users the opportunity at no cost to broadcast videos on the Internet. The video can be uploaded, tagged, and shared. It can also be used to view thousands of

original videos that were uploaded by community members. There are many video groups to connect with people of similar interests.

- ▶ **Atomic Learning (http://www.atomiclearning.com):** This site provides web-based training for assistive technology software and a few hardware devices. The training consists of short videos and demonstrations on how to use specific products. There are some free tutorials. A subscription fee is required to view the video tutorials based on use. Some offer closed captioning as an option.
- ▶ **Edublogs (http://www.Edublogs.tv):** This is an example of a great video blog to promote education. There is a great deal of video and audio for parents or teachers who want to explore more information on a variety of topics.

VIDEO PODCASTS
- ✓ This term is used when video is provided on demand.
- ✓ For a great example, check out Closing The Gap—Assistive Technology Resources for Children and Adults with Special Needs at http://www.podcast.tv/video-podcasts/closing-the-gap-assistive-technology-resources-for-children-and-adults-with-special-needs-144726.html.

WEB 2.0
- ✓ Web 2.0 is associated with web applications that facilitate interactive information sharing and collaboration when online.
- ✓ To learn about the many Web 2.0 applications go to http://www.go2web20.net.

WEBSITES
- ✓ A website is a collection of web pages all connected to the same home page.
- ✓ Some websites require a subscription to some or all of the contents while others offer open access. Some subscriptions are free and some require a fee.
- ✓ An example of a helpful website is Parents Helping Parents at http://www.php.com. It provides a great deal of very helpful information about parenting children with disabilities. There is a large amount of information about early intervention, identification, appropriate education, and support for parenting.

WEBSITE ACCESSIBILITY

✓ Website accessibility is becoming more important as Internet access becomes mainstream and more people with disabilities are learning to use assistive technology to obtain information and interact with online society.

✓ In the U.S., it is now the law that federally funded websites must be Section 508 compliant, or accessible to those with disabilities. More information on this law can be found at http://www.section508.gov.

✓ For more information about accessibility issues, check out http://www.w3.org/WAI.

WIKIS

✓ A wiki is a collaborative website comprised of the collective work of many authors.

✓ It allows users to easily upload, edit, and interlink pages.

✓ A popular wiki is Wikipedia (http://www.wikipedia.com)—an open content encyclopedia. It is offered in many languages.

✓ Another great wiki by Karen Janowski (an assistive and educational technology consultant) is about assistive technology for students: http://udltechtoolkit.wikispaces.com.

WRITING COLLABORATION IN REAL TIME

✓ These tools offer web-based word processing, synchronously.

✓ No sign up is required and the products can be used immediately.

✓ When multiple people edit the same document simultaneously, any changes are instantly reflected on everyone's screen. The result is a new and productive way to collaborate with text documents, which is useful for meeting notes, brainstorming, project planning, and training.

✓ Different authors are assigned their own colors.

✓ Many offer decent word processing capabilities including text alignment, undo/redo, text formatting, bullets, document import, and revision-based save.

✓ Most enable users to import and export documents.

  ▶ **TitanPad**: http://www.titanpad.com
  ▶ **PiratePad**: http://www.piratepad.net
  ▶ **Sync.in**: http://sync.in
  ▶ **Scribblar**: http://www.scribblar.com

CHAPTER 13

ADAPTED E-MAIL, SEARCH ENGINES, AND WEB BROWSERS

The Internet has changed the way many of us carry out everyday social, vocational, and leisure pursuits. It has become an integral part of our lives that permits us to take advantage of a wide range of tasks in an efficient and convenient way. Use of e-mail and the Internet can help link people with community, friends, and family. Online access provides a way to efficiently gather information.

The ability to use the Internet and e-mail is especially important for people with communication and cognitive deficits for a number of reasons. It offers:

- ✓ a means of communication for people who have difficulty talking;
- ✓ a written record of communication for people with memory issues;
- ✓ a practical, meaningful way to practice functional reading and writing skills;
- ✓ easier access to information; and
- ✓ an efficient way to plan and coordinate activities.

Many people with communication and cognitive challenges never try or initially fail with their attempts to use e-mail, instant messaging, electronic mailing lists, social networks, or chat room discussions. However, with the use of helpful tools and strategies, many people can successfully use these forms of communication.

STRATEGIES TO USE WITH ALREADY ESTABLISHED E-MAIL ACCOUNTS

✓ The therapist or teacher should produce printed communication sheets with tailored greetings, questions, and descriptions of daily activities that the user would send. The individual can then copy these sentences into the e-mail. The written information acts as a "social script" for communication. Templates are also useful.

✓ Develop designated computer files that contain questions, comments, and sentences to cut and paste for use in e-mail messages.

✓ Load a talking program such as WordQ or Universal Reader that will speak the messages aloud as they are typed. The auditory feedback often makes errors more noticeable at the time they are produced, which reduces the amount of editing that needs to be done at the end.

✓ Use word prediction software, a thesaurus, or a dictionary with relational links for people with word retrieval deficits to use while typing messages.

✓ Use a talking word processor that is compatible with e-mail to facilitate reading and writing.

✓ Configure the existing e-mail account if possible to make it more user friendly. Settings may allow users to increase the font size, automatically enter the password, read the next e-mail, and check the spelling.

ADAPTED E-MAIL PROGRAMS

As with other types of programs, adapted e-mail programs offer different features, including:

✓ the ability to send a message using recorded voice;

✓ the ability to send messages by selection of pictures to communicate a message;

✓ the use of pictures in the address book;

✓ a simplified user interface;

✓ text-to-speech technology that reads aloud incoming messages;

✓ speech recognition engines, so that spoken messages used to write the messages are converted to text as well as sent as a sound file attachment;

✓ simplification of sequencing of steps with spoken and visual prompts;

✓ self-contained e-mail groups;

✓ inclusion of training programs to learn to use the software; and
✓ inclusion of video messages.

E-MAIL USING RECORDED VOICE, VIDEO, OR PICTURES

Many people who are unable to read or write, but can speak intelligibly may benefit from voice-based e-mail systems or the use of voice-recognition products. E-mail that uses recorded voice can enable people who are dependent on devices to help them communicate via e-mail.

Coglink Email
by Think and Link
http://www.personaltechnologies.com

- This easy-to-use, personalized e-mail program is designed for individuals with significant cognitive impairments.
- It helps users build their own community of e-mail buddies. Only people on the correspondent list managed by the help desk can exchange messages.
- Users are protected from junk e-mail and viruses through the Coglink program.
- Coglink includes an automated training program that helps users learn all of the basic skills for using the mouse, keyboard, and e-mail.
- Coglink has several advanced features that can be added to the basic program at a later time. It comes with an easy-to-use Helper link that allows clinicians and care providers to instantly add, change, or remove advanced features.
- Windows and Mac
- $69.95 (one-time fee)

Eyejot
by Eyejot, Inc.
http://www.eyejot.com

- Eyejot is a feature-rich online video mail platform.
- Check the blog tab for the most recent information on the product.
- It works on almost any browser and operating system.
- The recipient does not need to have Eyejot to view the video.
- Users can select a message and press the View Recipients button to list everyone that received their Eyejot.

- Windows, Mac, iPad, and iPhone
- There are multiple versions of Eyejot, including a free one and a yearly subscription.

IcanEmail
by RJ Cooper & Associates
http://www.rjcooper.com

- This is a full-screen, talking e-mail program designed with a basic interface for users with cognitive, visual, and/or physical challenges.
- The program asks a series of questions, one at a time, to help the user sequence the steps.
- The user can speak messages, and the recorded voice is sent.
- The user controls word-by-word reading.
- Accessible with a single switch.
- The e-mail "partner" (the sender or recipient) can send and receive mail without any special software.
- Windows and Mac
- $119.00

Vemail
by NCH Software
http://www.nch.com.au/vemail

- This software allows the user to use ordinary e-mail to record a message instead of typing it. The message is compressed and sent as an attachment.
- Anyone can receive and listen to the Vemail. It can be played with the standard player installed in almost all computers.
- If a speech recognition engine is installed on the sender's computer, it will translate the recording into text and include it with the e-mail.
- This program can also be used to send and receive e-mail with a cell phone for $4.99 a month.
- Messages can be read using text-to-speech software and replied to with voice.
- Windows
- $19.99

Web Trek Connect
by AbleLink Technologies
http://www.ablelinktech.com

- This program provides a simplified picture-based system for both receiving and sending e-mail with standard e-mail programs. It uses photos and spoken prompts to guide the user through selecting an e-mail address and recording a spoken message, then sending the message.

- When receiving mail, the user needs only to click on the sender's picture to initiate the built-in screen reader or to automatically play an attached audio recording. The user's e-mail box can be set up so that it receives messages only from people in the address book.
- Windows
- $199.00 with the Computer & Web Access Suite

ADAPTED SEARCH ENGINES, WEB BROWSERS, AND MORE

Many web pages and search engines are too complex for users with communication and cognitive challenges. Most of the mainstream browsers are often inaccessible to people using text and screen readers. People with visual impairments or reading difficulties can benefit from special browsers or by customizing a mainstream browser to make it easier to see and use. Some offer text-to-speech, speech recognition, or alternate access modes. There is a growing movement to make mainstream browsers such as Chrome more accessible for people with disabilities.

Firefox
by Mozilla
http://www.mozilla.com

- Firefox is a free web browser that comes with many built-in features for customization through free add-ons.
- There are currently 5,000 free add-ons grouped by categories. The language support section includes add-ons such as: Google Dictionary and Translate (which offers in-line translation of any word the user points to or highlights or an entire page of a web page in another language); Fox Lingo (which offers web page and text translation, a dictionary, a grammar checker, and text-to-speech); and Text to Voice.
- There are many accessibility tools and features available at http://www.accessfirefox.org.
- It is available in different languages.
- Windows, Mac, and Linux
- Free

Google Accessible Search
by Google
http://labs.google.com/accessible
- Google has designed a web filter in which it prioritizes keyword search results according to a website's accessibility.
- Windows and Mac
- Free

KidZui
http://www.kidzui.com
- KidZui is a free web browser, search engine, and online playground for kids ages 3–12.
- Kids safely express themselves, with their Zui, backgrounds, tags, and online status.
- KidZui sends a weekly e-mail that tells parents what their kids are doing online. The KidZui parent account lets parents share content and set limits.
- KidZui Search is tailored to the needs of kids. Its search feature provides suggestions and spelling correction, search results with content relevant to kids, and graphical presentation that is easy for kids to understand.
- Windows and Mac
- Free

PACK Drive
by Think and Link
http://www.personaltechnologies.com
- PACK is a portable computing tool that includes a user-friendly desktop and four accessible programs on a self-launching U-3 Flash drive. PACK makes computer use accessible for people with cognitive impairments.
- Windows and Mac
- Contact company for pricing.

Readability
by arc90
http://lab.arc90.com/experiments/readability
- This is a tool to remove clutter (such as pictures and flashing advertisements) from web pages to make them easier to read.
- Users can choose the font and size of the text and the size of the margins.

- It works best on pages that have long sections of text.
- A bookmarklet (added to the browser's bookmark toolbar) must be clicked to remove the surrounding clutter.
- Apple users can just go to the website they want to read, click on the view menu, and then choose Safari Reader to use this product.
- Windows and Mac
- Free

Web Trek
by AbleLink Technologies
http://www.ablelinktech.com

- Web Trek is a picture-based browser that allows the user to capture a picture directly off of a web page and then displays the picture as a large button on the main Web Trek page.
- The website can then be accessed by clicking on the picture. Once the website is accessed, the site is navigated through its traditional link buttons.
- Large arrows are displayed for moving to the next or previous page.
- If the symbol mode is selected, the text is presented in a simplified display with symbols above the words; the user still sees the graphics on the site.
- Text mode presents the same simplified display without the symbols, although it still includes the graphics.
- The text can be converted to a preferred font that is easier to see and can be read aloud. The program speaks sentence by sentence, highlighting each word as it is spoken.
- Links can be spoken before they are selected. Webwide provides symbol support for text on web pages using Widgit Rebus symbols described at (http://www.widgit.com).
- $199.00 with the Computer & Web Access Suite

REFERENCES

Assistive Technology Act of 2004, P.L. 108-364, HR 4278.

Bright Solutions for Dyslexia. (1998). *What is dyslexia?* Retrieved from http://www.dys-add.com/define.html

Kurzweil Educational Systems. (n.d.). *How Kurzweil 3000 supports the principles of Universal Design for Learning.* Retrieved from http://www.kurzweiledu.com/files/Kurzweil%203000%20and%20UDL.pdf

National Center for Learning Disabilities. (2010). *Visual processing disorders.* Retrieved from http://www.ncld.org/ld-basics/related-issues/information-processing/visual-processing-disorders

ABOUT THE AUTHOR

Joan L. Green is a speech-language pathologist in the Washington, DC, area with many years of experience helping children and adults who have a wide range of communication, cognitive, literacy, and learning challenges. She has developed unique state-of-the-art local and long-distance therapy, coaching, and training programs for families and professionals. She is passionate in her efforts to spread the word about how affordable cutting-edge technology can be used to empower children and adults who have difficulty with speaking, reading, writing, thinking, and learning at home, school, work, or in the community. She authored *Technology for Communication and Cognitive Treatment: The Clinician's Guide* and coauthored the video eBook *Technology Supports for Writing*.

Joan offers live and recorded webinars as well as an informative free e-newsletter to more than 8,000 recipients that highlights technology goldmines and strategies for professionals and families to help maximize progress toward goals.

In 2008, she received the Most Outstanding Contribution to the Field award from the Maryland Speech-Language Hearing Association. Joan received her professional training at Northwestern University and is the mother of four. A listing of her therapy programs, description of her books and webinars, and information about her other services can be found at http://www.innovativespeech.com and http://www.ittsguides.com.